EMOTIONAL INTELLIGENCE

The complete guide on how to improve your social skills, empathy, self-confidence, and successful relationships.

Learn how to overcome depression and achieve a better life.

Robert Daniel Skill

Table of contents

CHAPTER 1
Relationship between emotions and empathy

The concept of emotions and empathy is a broad field which can be narrowed. The first step is to understand what these terms mean. Emotions can be defined as a negative or positive experience that correlates to a certain pattern of psychological doings. Empathy, on the other hand, is described as a person's ability to understand and share the feelings of other people. Empathy is a word originated from a German word Einfühlung that means feeling in.

A person is supposed to be aware of empathy so as to understand his or her emotional intelligence. Empathy will help a person respond to certain situations with ease. Such a situation will include handling a partner who came to the home with sad news from work. Therefore, it is integral parts in people's lives for over decades in begin of time. It helps people to connect and love other people surrounding them. There are several facets that are used to describe empathy in people's lives. Therefore, there are several ways identified by psychologists that people can feel empathy. These common ways include emotional, compassionate and cognitive empathy.

The emotional, cognitive and compassionate empathy have different ways of manifesting in life. The reflection they give is in different ways is always a manifestation of a person's day to day life. Life experience across family, work and friend have an influence of on the different manifestations ways. An individual will also notice the change when handling this set of people in his or her daily life. There are numerous examples in the current globe which are documented. The documentation can be accessed with availability of technology that has made the globe a small village.

Three Forms of Empathy

Cognitive Empathy

Cognitive empathy can also be described as a thought despite it being a form of emotion in people's lives. There are several ways people can understand what cognitive empathy is. It can be described as comprehending or understanding emotions on a higher intellectual level. Human beings have a complex brain that can be able to distinguish events. Therefore, most people can be able to comprehend that sadness is not similar to feeling sad.

The best elucidation can be driven by a hospital environment. The main focus in this set up would be aimed at a doctor and ailing patient. A doctor is trained to look for the cause of the illness in a patient without getting immersed in a patient's emotions. It is the same way a partner can react to his or her companion sharing bad news from work. The aim of cognitive emotions is to respond to situation by use of brain power. This the situation that people see other human beings as weird by the way they handle emotions. It is because different situation makes different sense to different people.

This type of empathy is a very important tool in the current social set up. The form of cognitive empathy helps a person to penetrate inside another person's mind while conversing. This form of empathy also helps people to have tact conversation with deep understanding levels. Some people can relate this ideology with the thought or action of mixing oranges and apples. The thought can be further expanded in a way that; to truly understand another person's feelings, one just needs to understand the emotions without diving in them. However, people who practice this type of empathy risk a situation to be referred to as cold people.

Emotional Empathy

Emotional empathy is a direct thought from the way it is referred by its name. The process involved a direct feeling of another person's emotions by an individual. People with this ability are commonly referred to as empaths. These people are very unique since their ability transcends to fully taking into consideration other people metal state and what they feel. Empaths are used to the words used by several people of having a lot of feelings while in bad mental states.

This form of empathy may look like it has a disconnect from the brain and the thinking. However, it is a form of empathy that has deep roots in the reflection of human beings neurons. Animals across the globe have neurons which have a certain way when they react in moments they see other animals act. Emotional empathy is able to obtain the same feeling another person experience in the same situation present.

The best example can be depicted by couples in a relationship. A good partner is supposed to be able to feel the emotional state his or her partner is in when the partner comes home crying. It can be associated with the natural response that pulls people heartstrings. The process can be very important in a person's life because it has the potentials of creating deep relationship bonds which are intimate. Emotional empathy has its downsides a person seeking emotional intelligence is supposed to understand. Feeling so much of other people can make small interactions look overwhelming.

Compassionate Empathy

This form of empathy is ideal in the current world and it has been effective over the years. Compassionate form of empathy is very helpful when people hold talks about political or monetary talks and meetings. It is always the first form of response people show their children and their loved ones. People use it to get a balance in their relationships too. People have a similar relationship between what they feel at heart and what they think in the brain. The best thing about compassionate empathy is the fact it honors natural connection.

A good example can be illustrated in the relationship between couples. A partner seeks to understand the situation makes a partner cry. He or she goes further to comforting the lover after getting a clear insight. This a balance achieved from complimenting emotional empathy and cognitive empathy. This form of empathy seeks to improve a person emotional intelligence. Having a fit emotional state can enable a person to can help a person at home, at work and in other social places.

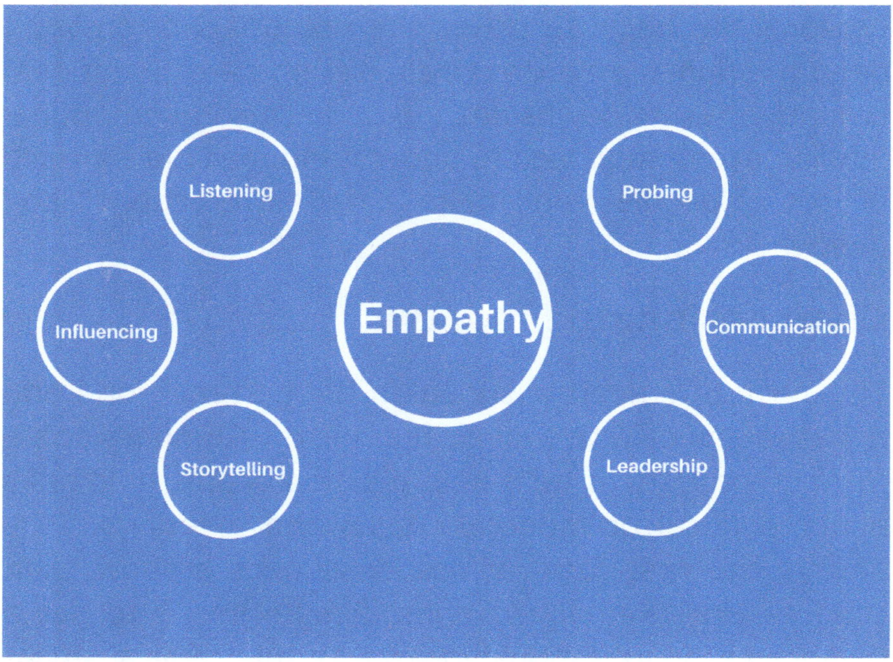

CHAPTER 2
Emotional intelligence

It is a common occurrence in human being lives when they look back at important decisions made and question oneself. Questions that tend to crisscross a person's mind are what he or she was thinking or why he or she had to do that. These situations bring the rise of the emotional intelligence idea. It is an important tool in the day to day life of a human being because it helps a person overcome regrets.

Emotional intelligence can easily be understood as the ability of an individual to identify, understand, use and control emotions. This process is supposed to be done in a calm manner to make it have a positive and effective impact. A person who has high emotional intelligence has various advantages in the current life. He or she is able to have better communication with people, resolve conflicts, improve his or her relationships and reduce anxiety levels in their lives. Having high emotional intelligence helps a person have high empathy levels which are critical in relationships.

People's emotional intelligence has a big potential for people having quality life. It is because it is an influential factor in how people behave. People with incredible level of good behavior are associated with healthy relationships that promote quality life a person's lives. High level of emotional intelligence is commonly associated with improved levels of self-awareness. These qualities bring different states in a person's life since a person has purpose, autonomy and intention which are components of a quality life

A greater part of the global community is heavily affected by the process of decision making. Several people make decisions anchoring them of the current happenings and circumstances. The thought that cloud people during these complicated situations is if the perception that things are beyond the ability to be changed. The impact these thoughts give is an individual's mind is the limited amount of options and solutions. Therefore, an individual is advised to take time to reflect over these scenarios. Reflecting helps a person to examine what on the issue and come up with the best ways the situation can be handled.

Developing an individual's emotional intelligence quotient has a greater influence on an individual's life to success. An emotional quotient is a standard form used by psychologist used in determining a person's emotional intelligence. The process is greatly influenced by a person's personal situation and his or her intelligence. The impact of high emotional quotient is felt in several aspects of an individual's life. It cuts through how a person makes his choices, finds solutions and creates other options when situations are difficult. There are several ways a person can improve his or her emotional quotient.

Ways to Cultivate Emotional Quotient

Self-Awareness

Self-awareness can be described as the ability of an individual to recognize, label and get a clear understanding of his or her emotions. A person is supposed to know he or she is supposed to work with before initiating the change in his or her life. The process helps a person to get a finer understanding of his emotions and know the result it gives to people in the surrounding. Various sportsmen have undergone the pieces of training to be self-aware so as to conquer their emotions.

A person who is self-aware has the ability to know his or her strengths. Process of knowing one's strength helps a person knows his or her limits and how to improve them. Individuals in this form of information instilled in their daily life practices are often confident. Their level of confidence cuts across what they are capable of and those things they can't do. This helps a person to be assertive in what he or she chooses to believe in during the day to day life. Being assertive can be confused with the phenomenon of getting whatever people want anytime.

Being self-aware and assertive helps a person to justify his or decision without regrets when faced with difficult situations. The presence of satisfactory justification to ideas helps people to get closure of difficult life happenings. An individual can improve his or her awareness by rating him or herself, asking people surrounding him or her on the feedback of the behavior he or she has and tasking him or herself with a complete formal assessment test. This process is a key factor for emotional quotient increase.

Emotional Regulation

The process of regulating emotions involves an individual's ability to manage his or her strong emotions. The process is successful when a person does not react in a destructive way on raw emotions. Emotional regulation helps to reduce stress levels and improves a person's emotional intelligence. It is because an individual will have the ability to sit down with unwanted emotion and give him or herself time to decide on the best action to take over the situation. Taking time helps a person calm and get back to his or her senses which is critical while making important decisions.

Emotional regulation gives a person the potential of considering several solutions to a problem. This, in turn, improves a person's emotional intelligence because an individual won't base his decision to a single thought. It leads to improvement of a person's emotional quotient by having better ability in making decisions.

Empathy

It is easy to develop deep and more intimate relationships with people surrounding us when we can empathize with them. Empathy is simply having the ability to recognize other people's feeling. One of the good things about this quality is that it helps people to anticipate actions. Therefore, people are able to portray good behavior while handling fellow human beings and how we influence them. It helps a person improves his or her personal relationships with people around him or her. Good levels of handing people are always associated with having high emotional quotient.

Social Skills

The term socials skill is a broad term in the current globe. However, it can be generalized as the ability of a person to communicate in a clear, courteous and concise manner to people around him or her. An individual with high levels of social skills includes having topnotch self-awareness, good empathy levels and implacable emotional regulation. It is a summation of high emotional quotient.

CHAPTER 3
The brain chemistry of emotions, how ei can improve it

The human brain is a complex network that is active each and every second processing huge quantities of information. The network section of the human brain is responsible for processing include neurons. Neurons simply refer to the cells that are responsible for signal transmission throughout the brain. To send these signals, neurons use neurotransmitters which basically are chemicals some being released while others are received. It is these chemicals that facilitate effective communication between the different parts of the brain. The neurotransmitters or the chemical that affects human emotions include norepinephrine, dopamine and serotonin. Norepinephrine is a neurotransmitter responsible for moderating and controlling anxiety and stress. Dopamine is a neurotransmitter that gives you the experiences of pleasure and learning. This means that when you have some pleasurable experience that makes you happy, dopamine teaches your brain to have the desire to do this particular experience more and more or again and again. Lastly, serotonin is a neurotransmitter that is responsible for easing depression. This means that serotonin level imbalance can make you feel depressed, anxious and angry.

Your emotions can be affected if there are abnormalities in the way your brain is receiving and processing these chemicals. A good example is if your brain has abnormalities with the section interacting with chemical dopamine. Dopamine, as we have already discussed, relate to pleasurable experiences and rewards learning. Therefore, when you are involved in an activity that is rewarding or pleasurable, you will feel less happy or you may likely feel sad for an activity that you should have been happy. Many people suffering from major depressive disorder (MDD) have been found to have fewer receptors for serotonin neurotransmitters in their brains.

Looking Deep into the Chemicals Linked with Our Emotion

Emotions are generally very complex and will mean differently to different people. Emotions refer to a conscious experience that is determined by the states of mind, expressions and internal and external reactions. As humans, we have so many emotions. Just to look at a few, we have, anger, depression, love, sadness, jealousy, passion, apathy, sorrow, frustration, pleasure, happiness, pride, annoyance, confidence, hope etc.

Emotions can be described based on how we feel. The arousal of our nervous system creates different emotions in us. At any given time, there are millions of chemical reactions taking place in our brains. These chemical reactions are as a result of synapses. Through synapses, neurotransmitters in the neurons of the nervous system transmit messages. We can measure emotions in our physiological responses. For instance, we can measure our emotions based on the pounding of our hearts, the adrenaline release, blood rushing to the face and sweating. The expression can also be seen as a major part of emotion. The parts of the nervous system that can be associated with expression include the brain stem, the limbic system and major cortex. The amygdala and the frontal cortex are parts of the nervous system affecting the emotion the most. The amygdala associates with emotions like feeling sad, angry and afraid. The frontal cortex on the other hand associated with emotions like feeling happy and feeling pleasure.

Throughout the day, we tend to experience many different emotions. In many times, these emotions are always transient in nature. However, when these emotions become very negative, our behaviors as well as our biochemistry can be dramatically affected. Our emotions are basically controlled by certain brain areas as well as the different chemicals present in our brains. Here are the chemicals that help our bodies to work normally and how their balance affects our emotions and moods.

ix. Dopamine

Dopamine is released by the hypothalamus. Dopamine is associated with happiness, alertness, cognition, vigilance and memory. Having low dopamine levels in your body can make you feel depressed, have mood swings, have cognitive problems, low or no satisfaction is activities of our daily lives, low attention and even have compulsive behavior. Again, high levels of dopamine can lead to an individual having a suspicious personality and addictive behaviors. If you have low levels of dopamine in your brain, consider eating foods rich in phenylalanine and tyrosine like milk, turkey, eggs and cheese because they have amino acids.

x. Serotonin

Serotonin is responsible for regulating biological and physiological function like feelings of arousal, moods, your thinking abilities and feelings of aggression. When you have the right levels of serotonin, you will have feelings related to uplifted moods and feeling relaxed. When you have high levels of serotonin, you will feel apathy and sedated. On the other hand, low levels of serotonin are associated with poor control of appetite, feeling depressed, having sexual problems, low mood, poor social skills and poor appetite control. Disruption in levels of in serotonin in the brain is also associated with mood disorders, anxiety disorders and depression. To enhance serotonin production, you can try meditation as it inhibits the regions of the brain producing stress.

xi. Acetylcholine

This hormone is released from never endings (the ends of the peripheral and central nervous system). It is the primary neurotransmitter and is in charge of movements of muscles, memory, concentration and alertness. Optimal levels of acetylcholine results in elevated moods focused mind and increased intelligence. Acetylcholine is also responsible for the control of primitive drives and emotions including being aggressive, having fear and being angry. When there is an imbalance of Acetylcholine levels in the neurotransmitters, the primitive and drives can affect you and the people around you.

xii. Oxytocin

This hormone is made in the hypothalamus. Oxytocin plays a crucial role in an individual's pro-social behavior. Generally, the release of Oxytocin evokes feelings including feeling contented, feeling calm and anxiety reduction by inhibiting the sections of the brain responsible for controlling anxiety, fear and protection against stress. Increase in levels of oxytocin makes an individual have increased trust, social interaction and empathy. Oxytocin deficiency is associated with pathophysiology of feeling depressed, having poor communication skills, being irritative, having disturbed sleep, feeling more anxious and having fears.

xiii. Gamma-aminobutyric acid (GABA)

GABA is a brain activity regulator. It is produced in from glutamic acid. It is an inhibitory neurotransmitter that slows down the limbic system activity thus reducing fear, panic and anxiety. In other words, GABA acts like natural tranquilizer suppressing prolactin. The hormone prolactin is responsible for stimulating night time incontinence.

xiv. Norepinephrine and epinephrine

Norepinephrine acts both as a neurotransmitter and a hormone. Norepinephrine is responsible for arousing the brain and the sympathetic nervous system. It is responsible for increasing blood pressure and breathing rate and is released by adrenal glands. As a hormone, Norepinephrine is responsible for fight or flight responses in relation to the body stress. Epinephrine, on the other hand, is released by the medulla of the adrenal glands and is specifically released at the times of emergency and fear. Epinephrine provokes responses to stress and arouses extreme emotions such as amusement, anger or fear. It has been observed that too little amounts of norepinephrine and epinephrine associates with depression while high levels of norepinephrine and epinephrine associated with mood disorders such as schizophrenia.

How can emotional Intelligence improve the brain chemistry of emotions?

The following are the personal competencies stemming from the concept of emotional intelligence. Generally, no one would be able to score 100% of these qualities. However, you can strengthen your limitations. For you to achieve outstanding performance, you must have five essential domains including social skills of an individual, awareness of the self, self-motivation, self-regulation and having empathy.

i. Self-awareness

Awareness of the self basically entails having knowledge and understanding about the internal states about yourself, intuitions and your preferences. It basically involves being; emotionally aware by recognizing your emotions as well as the effects of these emotions; accurately assessing yourself -by knowing your strengths and limited, and having self-confidence - knowing your self-worth as well as capabilities.

ii. Self-regulation

Self-regulation involves how you manage your internal resources and impulses. This includes: Having self-control where you are able to check your impulses and disruptive emotions; having a feeling of trustworthiness where you are able to maintain high standards of integrity and honesty; having a sense of conscientiousness where you are responsible for your personal performance; and adaptability which means that you are flexible in handling changes.

iii. Social Skills

Social Skills means that you are an individual with adeptness and you are able to provide desirable responses to the people around you. Working on your social skills means that you will be able to influence or persuade others, clearly communicate in an open and convince manner; be able to manage conflicts; participate in group works and be able to build bonds.

iv. Empathy

Empathy means that you are aware of the feelings of other people. This means that you are able to understand others, being able to develop others, being able to leverage diversity and being able to read the current emotional currents.

Motivation

This means that you are an individual with emotional tendencies guiding or facilitating you to reach your goals. You are able to achieve an inner drive, be committed, and be optimistic.

Understanding these five essential domains emotional intelligence can help you improve the brain chemistry of emotions because you will respond rather than react even when faced with emotionally charged situations. With the five skills, you will be able to respond rather than react and get defensive. Emotional intelligence approach will tell you to keep calm, get the perspective of the situation, before judging, listen and hold yourself from reacting head-on. Secondly, you will show up with your real self. Most people tend to hide who they are especially when they are faced with hard situations or people. When you are emotionally intelligent, you will be able to present yourself with integrity and emotional transparency. Emotional intelligence will help you to think before speaking, practice self-control, look at the whole picture of an even thus you will be able handle tough or difficult situations better. These are all factors that will enable you to be in control of all your emotions thus be in control of your brain chemistry.

CHAPTER 4
Impact of emotional intelligence on families

As defined earlier, emotional intelligence is said to the capability of identifying and managing one`s emotions and those of others. Emotional intelligence comprises three different skills; awareness of the emotions and the ability to harness those emotions and harness them, it affects even the family life of an individual. It is worth noting that the ability to manage and identify emotions is critical in helping others do so. In other words, if you are living in a family, you may need to have such intelligence and support those you are related to being in a position of identifying and managing such emotions. The aspect increases love, cohesion, and allows family members to work together as a team.

Growth of Children

Developmental theories explain that during the adolescence stage, an individual is able to develop some critical formation in life that is essential in the latter days. Although a lesser role I perceived to these teenagers at this age, family life plays a pivotal role in the development of these young guys. In most cases, the young are able to gain physical, emotional as well as cognitive independence during this age. It is worth noting that during this stage, there is a dire need of maintaining a balance between the home environment and the world for the teenage to be intelligent in all aspects. Such experiences are critical in the sense that they allow the kids to stay in their families and adore the lessons they learn as they are growing. If parents are sensitive, this is the best time to strike some sense of unity and unequivocal devotion that are sensitive in life. A child is able to adapt some of the knowledge critical in esteeming life differently. The occurrences in life at this stage are essential in the sense that they strike a changeability and affable that enhances individuals to interact with conventions as well as family ties. It is during this stage that individuals are able to tests and identify some of these tips that are critical in handling problems. In most cases, when an individual isn't able to identify a particular emotion, he or she might develop some difficulties that tend to affect their approach to issues. In cases such tips or attitudes towards life aren't prepared at this stage, the teenager might have a problem in identifying and managing some of these emotions.

Enhances More Connection

Even if people are born in the same families, they tend to behave differently act differently and maybe approach things differently. Their emotions tend to differ, and they perceive and understand things differently. However, having different approaches in life doesn't necessarily mean that they cannot live together. What enhances this unity is the art of understanding and managing their emotions in the right way. A man might be having some issues with the other family members. For instance, he might be furious about a duty that wasn't conducted well. However, if the woman in the family can identify the emotion in the man and manage it calmly, the family will keep living together in harmony. Thus, the art of understanding how one feels as well as their nature in life is critical in the sense that it helps families to live in unity. If you are able to identify some of the reasons that causes one to feel pissed off in life, you will automatically avoid them. In other words, emotional intelligence helps one learn different ways of living with other people without affecting their emotions negatively.

Become a Better Communicator

In families, communication is critical. However, when communicating, it is good to consider the emotion of friends as well as those you are speaking to. Your body language, tone, as well as the intonation used, determines the effectiveness of communication. It is worth noting that in most cases, people develop ways of communicating to individuals as well as methods of encoding emotions as they grow. Thus, if the individuals are able to encode information from any speaker as they grow, the art of being better speakers tend to develop as well. In other words, better speakers learn the art of understanding emotions as they grow.

Being a better Leader

Even in families, leadership is critical. The art of leadership with emotional intelligence entails the desires and the abilities to influence others. One of the biggest mistakes that some owners of the families do is to dictate the way things should be conducted without considering the emotions of their family members. Such approaches to life tend to affect the way the members of these families relate to each other. In other words, if you want to become a better leader, you need to develop some emotional intelligence that will help you understand the feeling of your fellow-subjects. In other words, you need to have some information that will help you influence others without affecting their feelings negatively. Learn to appreciate how each person feels in regards to anything that cuts across their minds. With emotional intelligence, you will be in a position of understanding what people desire in life as well as the way of handling their concerns. The aspect allows one to be charismatic and lead with a good example.

If you want to increase your credibility, you need to learn how to deal with different individuals with the way they handle issues. Thus, you need to develop some emotional intelligence within yourself so as you can be able to gain more credibility among those you lead. People with emotional intelligence are less depressed. They are able to perform their duties well in their families and lead an exemplary life. Thus, emotional intelligence plays a critical role in boosting the unity among families and enhance more cohesions. As you bring up your families, try and equip some of these aspects in life and help them learn how to encode emotions from different people. Such elements will help them live happily with their friends and relatives in the future.

You can appreciate your family

An emotionally intelligent person can easily recognize the good in the other person. And as well know when they do not enjoy the same. Immediately you realize that you appreciate your family as you should, correct that as soon as possible. You will know when the other family member has made a mistake unintentionally. And for this, you will not get into an assumption that they did that to annoy you. You will place your confidence to someone even though you are not sure whether they are sincere. For example, you can request your partner to bring you a specific item, and instead, they bring you a different thing. That may be a way to show that probably they did not care or consider your feelings. Instead of showing how you are hurt by what you have done, let them know that you still believe in them. Assume that they did not get the exact thing that you required, but they made an effort to bring you which is close to your specification. It will not lead to a completely different outcome rather than an argument.

Feelings are recognized as well as acknowledged

Both the negative and positive emotions are subject to being looked at attentively, and the approaches to handle them expertly be laid down. You should let your children know that unpleasant feelings like anger should be expected in any situation because they are healthy. How you handle those feelings will determine whether there will be harmony in the family or not. An emotionally intelligent parent will teach their children the strategies to use to cool themselves down in such situations. They need to know how to determine the action they need to take to deal with a problem once they calm down. Teaching children through conversation as well as examples of how to live emotionally intelligent is vital. Teaching children emotional intelligence ways will play an important role to reduce the number of kids who wrestle with overeating. The level of destructive practices will go down because of seeing things from a positive point of view.

Nurture optimism as well as embrace realism

An emotionally intelligent family has an idea of how to take care of positivity as well as optimism. They not only recognize but also accept reality. They believe in themselves that they can go through tough times and emerge victoriously. The spirit of isolation is not given a chance in the family. They perceive they pose what it takes to set up an active family. Each one is ready to help the other in times of need and learn from their experiences. They view life from a positive perspective and do not let anything negative that has happened to ruin their harmony as a family. There is much happiness contributed by each person within the family.

Children are involved in decision making

The ideas of the children, as well as their opinion, are counted as a valid contribution. Both formal and informal meetings are held regularly in a family set up. Give your children the freedom to share their thought as well as ideas while you guide them. Though having a good argument is allowed, lay down policies on how to bring forth productive opinions. Children should learn how to think for themselves, and they are given an equal opportunity without dictating how things should be. Listening to your children as they give their opinion will help create a bond between you and them. You can know what their feelings are and as well be there to help them when they need you most.

CHAPTER 5
Impacts of emotional intelligence in a relationship

You will have a good rapport with one another

Empathy is one of the best indicators of emotional intelligence, and it is vital in making a relationship. Recognizing, as well as prioritizing your partners need, has a significant effect on whether your connection will be a healthy one or not. For togetherness felt between you and your partner, you need to do away with your priorities. Try and get yourself into your partner's shoes and to understand how they are feeling. Being tuned in to one another is an excellent way to of creating as well as deepening your bond. It helps you to understand the other person's emotions better in different situations. It will aid you relating to circumstance as well as factors resulting in either emotional reactions, residual thoughts or behavior. For example, you can ask questions to the other persona and as well seek their opinion. You will know where they stand by the kind of feedback they give. Do not make any comment or either a statement that will make them feel rejected.

You can engage in a critical conversation with an assurance that it will not escalate.

Someone who is emotionally intelligent is in a position to receive criticism unquestionably. Positive criticism is, at times, healthy in a relationship, and it matters. If received negatively and ends up into a fight, it will block some vital communication. Accepting to be criticized by you other partner is evidence that you are willing to learn as well as grow. Do not feel either blamed or attacked, instead take that as a chance to understand as well as learn. That will aid you to keep your feelings under control. You need to grow together with your partner to maintain a healthy relationship. Be willing to learn what is in you that your partner loves and what you need to work on, on their behalf. You will work on sharpening those skills when you have emotional intelligence. Embrace constructive feedback as well as try and make the relevant changes without being either defensive or taking issues personally.

An example is a case where you have done something thinking that you will be appreciated. Instead, the other person views that as a waste of time and resources too. Do not jump into a conclusion when told that was not the best thing to do. Seek to know why it was not a good idea to invest in such a thing. Do not allow anger to clip in before you hear the reason of being criticized. When the aim of being criticized is genuine, take that positively and change to better for next time.

You will express what you feel directly

Passive aggressiveness is an indication that one lack emotional intelligence. Applying silent treatment in a relationship to deal with conflicts is dangerous and can lead to the death of a relationship. You need to say what your feelings are as well as what you mean by everything you say. Do this verbally and respectively to have your requirement dealt with correctly. You need to speak up what is inside you. Your relationship will remain healthy when you share what your feelings are as well as ask for anything that you require from your partner. Your need will continue unmet when you do not express it. Being emotionally intelligent will help both you and the other party to avoid as well as reduce the passive-aggressive behavior. You don't have to remain silent and shut down all communication as a way of trying to put your point across. Speak out what you need and as well as work and respect the needs of the other person. Practice responding than reacting as well as focus on your attention and consider in what manner to behave. You will think about how to deal with the things that emotionally trigger you before you react. Do not forget that the first three minutes when you get into a conversation will determine it all. When you start a conversation in a harsh tone, the outcome will end up being miserable.

For example, when easily angered, you will end up throwing your temper to your partner as a way of dealing with stress. Consider thinking about what you will do the next moment you find yourself in a similar situation. Maybe you can tell your partner that you need some time alone to deal with your stress to avoid being volatile. Having some silent moment apart will help you calm down.

You find it easy to apologize as well as make amends quickly

An emotionally intelligent person will swallow their pride as well as admit they were wrong after a confrontation. You need to have the capability to apologize and as well make up immediately. That will help you to avoid building resentment, which can end up poisoning your relationship. Be quick to apologize when you do wrong, and you will avoid creating a distance between the bot of you and as well maintain your connection. Being emotionally intelligent will make you take ownership as well as have the desire to make amends quickly once you realize you have made a mistake. Barriers can be broken between partners as well as helping them understand each other. Engaging in a fruitful argument brings people together, and a case that escalates leads to the death of a relationship. Nurture as well as pay attention to your emotional intelligence.

No person is perfect, and the same case applies to both of you. Time and time again, you will have rough encounters or even do contrary to what your partner intended. When it gets to such a situation, put aside your pride and seek forgiveness. Apologizing defines a decent human being, and it will do more good than harm. Make changes as soon as possible and avoid in future making a similar mistake.

You find it comfortable to open up quickly to the other partner

You need to know the reasons why you are holding back. Being vulnerable will help you get attached to the other person with ease since you give yourself the freedom to feel one another. Don't shield yourself so much from the other person and with that you will connect easily. When you are emotionally intelligent, you will be conscious of how to deal as well as when to put down your guard. You tend to lose the connection when you start worrying about what you will do next as well as what you will do better. Don't ignore your partner's emotions; instead, take great care of them. Suppressing the other person's feelings will break the connection that you have making things to worsen. Trying to do away with emotions won't yield positive results because you can't control them. Unsolved issues between both of you will lead you to react emotionally. In such an instant, consider taking a deep breath or either pen down what you are experiencing and maybe the possible reason. Writing down will help you know what triggered your emotions and the best approach to use in dealing with each.

Time and again, we find ourselves in stressful situations, and we prefer not to share our burdens with people. A problem half shared is a problem half solved.

Opening up will ease the pain that is build up in you. It is also a sign that you trust as well as appreciate the presence of the other person. When your partner confides in you, take your time to understand what they are going through. They will feel secure knowing that they can count on you in case of anything. Sometimes it is when you feel offended by the other person. It is important to share out where they went wrong and find a way to rectify instead of keeping all you think to yourself. Opening up will only strengthen the bond between you and connection regained where it was lost.

Emotional intelligence helps someone stay committed

Staying committed maintains a healthy relationship and helps it to remain intact. You will understand the pain associated with losing fidelity as well as how devastating it feels to lose a partner. Respect will be the core thing that will make you stay faithful. You will honor your partner need as well as wishes and stand by them no matter what. Always appreciate the distinctive qualities, abilities as well as achievements of one another either verbally or nonverbally. A friend never betrays one other; instead, they provide support as well as care. Mutual affection binds them together since friendship is the principle thing to nurture a good relationship. Emotionally intelligent people understand one another perfectly in terms of what they like, as well as they dislike. They form a perfect pair of companions as well as confidants. Being unfaithful is being cruel to the other party. Someone who is emotionally intelligent will not allow any other relationship come between them and the partner.

You will stay humble always

Believing that you are better than the other person will get you emotional because of the things not meeting your expectations. View thing from a different angle instead of judging your partner. Put yourself in their position and find out whether you would have the same feeling and why. Being emotionally intelligent will make you see your shortcomings. You will understand your partner's thoughts as well as emotions in a broader way. Seek to learn how to handle a similar situation in a different way. Be humble and know that you are no better than the other person. You are different from everyone else around you.

CHAPTER 6
Impact of emotional intelligence at work

Emotional intelligence is understanding personal emotions and attitude and the ability to control them.
World Economic forum listed emotional intelligence as the sixth out of the top ten skills that employees require to thrive at work. Emotional intelligence is the ability to understand and control personal emotions and attitude. Emotional intelligence further gives a person the ability to understand other people's feelings. Social skills are also a part of emotional intelligence, and they help in building relationships at work and maintaining networks. A company's first success is derived from an excellent relating team.

Emotional intelligence is essential to both employers and employees. For Employers, decisions like who they hire, promote, and the fire is greatly influenced by their emotional intelligence. Employers and leaders in workplaces need EI to help them avoid making wrong managerial decisions. Having a high EI will save an employer recruitment costs because an employer can retain employees for long. Employees are loyal and work hard for an employer who shows understanding and compassion, which are the qualities of an employer with a high EI. It is essential, therefore, to have both employers and employees with Emotional Intelligence to make a working environment that is favorable to all.

Employees With High EI Are Most Sought Because Of The Following Reasons:

- Self-motivating – employees with high EI are their motivation and therefore always get the work done. With these kinds of employees, an organization's goals are easily achieved. Emotional intelligence extends from personal achievements to group achievements. Team playing, therefore, becomes smooth and success at work.
- Mental toughness – EI people respect others opinion at all times. This is because they have come to terms with the fact that they are not always right. Team playing at work requires mental toughness so that every person's opinion is put into consideration for better results. A working environment that has colleagues who have empathy for each other produces the best results.
- Productivity – a team that has EI is highly productive. This is because employees uplift each other. One worker will note a fault from their colleague, point it out to them, and in turn, the said person will positively consider the changes. EI people accept individual success as the group's and also the group's success is equally and fairly celebrated.

- Creating a friendly environment – everyone wants to work at a place where they always look forward to reporting to the next day. EI people have good relations with each other, which make work enjoyable. EI people look at their colleagues as family and therefore always strive to make each other happy.
- Efficiency – EI people are super-efficient in their work. They take everything seriously because they owe their reputation the success. At work, they give a 100percent performance because they have everything at heart.
- Decision making – EI consider the consequences of all decisions related to their work. They consider taking risks and how the failure to not take risks will affect their work. Before any decision is implemented, they will discuss amongst themselves and reach a conclusive decision that will favor everyone at work. Without EI decisions made tend to be controlling and unfavorable to some people. EI, therefore, allows people to be part of the decision making so that no one feels left out or disregarded.
- Solutions - In case things don't go as planned, resolutions are easily got. EI people always have a backup plan because they have evaluated situations before they happen. They are aware that things may not work out as planned, and when they do not, they know how to solve. Making solutions is not easy for people

with low EI because they use the time to throw blame games at each other.

- Customer service – EI know how to show empathy. Therefore, they can satisfy the customers because they can understand how the clients feel and understand what they need. Customers want to feel valued and appreciated, and EI knows how to deliver this.
- Handling pressure – EI people understand that every day is not the same. Some days will be hard and other days easy. EI people can keep their calm during hard times. Patience is very vital because failure to it more significant damages may be done. People with EI can easily handle their demanding bosses, annoying colleagues, and impatient customers.
- Personal conflicts – dealing with personal conflicts amongst colleagues is easy because you already understand each other's weaknesses. One can avoid heated moments with colleagues because they can walk away before things escalate. You can follow someone's emotions and therefore, able to relate well with them.
- Responding to criticism – an EI understands that the only feelings they can manipulate are theirs. They are, therefore, able to accept the negative and positive criticism without taking offence. Reflect on what they could have done differently, and change. An EI is not always critical of others,

and when they are, it is because the criticism is genuine. Therefore when they receive criticism themselves, they are willing to work on it.

It is not just about having EI but putting it into use is equally important. Below are ways of using EI at work:

1. Being self-aware – one has to be aware of their own emotions. To realize how they feel about specific issues and workmates, so that is easy to deal with them. Being aware of how you think and your limits will help you learn how to respond to issues differently. You will learn how to communicate better so that if making presentations was previously hard, you can now confidently do it. If your boss is stressful or your colleagues aren't too accommodating, you can calm yourself instead of making hasty decisions.

2. Regulation – controlling how you react and feel. You don't always have to be triggered by small things. One has to learn how to manage themselves in regards to nothing is permanent, and no matter how bad it is, it will pass regardless. Being able to control yourself will make you quickly adapt to changing situations. Most times, change is hard, but when you can control how you react towards change, it's easy. Some ways to self-regulate include:

    - Getting techniques to release stress from work. This will involve having extra activities outside work that you enjoy.

- Being calm is also a great technique because you understand that you can't control everything.
- Consideration of the consequences of doing something is a good regulator. Reacting without thinking it through will make a situation worse than it could have been.

3. Social skills – improving social skills will lead to excellent communication in the workplace. Passing and receiving information within the workplace is essential. Deadlines will be met, procrastination will be avoided, and a repeat of already done work will not happen. Communicating effectively within a group will lead to a strong team. Social skills help determine the most deserving leader within an organization. They are several ways to go about this:

    a. Listening to different opinions and suggestions by, asking a question, providing feedback, and getting feedback. People want to be involved in matters that interest them, and this is a great way.

    b. Paying attention to non-verbal communication – this will give you the real feel of what people at work think about you. You could be laying out an idea they don't agree on but are not communicating it through. Their nonverbal communication will help you assess their thoughts.

c. Avoiding drama in the office is an excellent technique of EI. Don't be that employee always fighting with everyone. Some arguments can be avoided when we control how we react.

4. Showing empathy – placing yourself into someone else's shoes. This will make you consider how they will feel when you do something to them. It is not just understanding how others feel but also showing empathy by how you react towards them. Sometimes it is hard to show compassion, especially when you think that someone is wrong, but since you want to avoid further conflicts, you decide to show empathy. It also involves letting others know that you value their contributions so that all parties can easily compromise.
5. Finding motivation – this does not include money or status but something more significant. Successful people do not place their motivation on this because failure to get this can demotivate them. Having a great attitude towards what you do is a great motivation. This is because you will always have something to look forward to. The right position can be gotten from finding the one thing you like about your work and focusing on it.

In a workplace where interpersonal relations are needed, Emotional Intelligence is much advocated for.

For employers, managers, supervisors, and any leader in a workplace, the ability to deal with staff is a great trait. Leaders should be able to treat employees with respect and encourage them to succeed. Emotional intelligence will help leaders know how to relate with the employees and therefore gain better results. Leaders can show empathy to their subordinates and build trust with them. When there is trust between the leaders and employees, work is more transparent. Leaders can manage the employees and enjoy their managerial role when there are issues between the two; it's easy to solve because a leader with emotional intelligence understands that mistakes happen. These kinds of leaders approach issues intelligently without disrespecting the staff. It's easy for leaders with EI to listen to and accept their junior's opinion without negatively criticizing the efforts of the employees. Employers with EI understand the need to reward deserving employees and are, therefore, able to motivate others to work hard.

CHAPTER 7
Impact of emotional intelligence on friendship

Emotional Intelligence refers to the process in which an individual is able to carry out themselves in a mature manner even at the face of overwhelming emotions. These are individuals who are able to contain pressure. They do this by either channeling the pressure to a positive aspect in life or either focusing rather on not concentrating emotions but rather choosing to ignore what you hear. These kinds of people have a desire to focus on devising a solution to a problem and attempting to dispose it at its onset. They take accountability for their actions no matter how severe the consequences might be.

A relationship is an arrangement that is built upon emotions. In a relationship, knowing how to respond to a different kind of pressure is what keeps the fire burning. There are a number of factors that act as pointers to emotional maturity. These include: Emotionally mature individuals in a relationship will always make a follow up to the other party in order to find out their headway. They are always keen about what is happening in their friend's life and even go a notch higher to remember and inquire about their progress.

For instance, your friend has been approaching a very important stage in his or her life, it could be education-wise or maybe a job interview thus something that will influence an individual's life positively. These kinds of friends will always make time to check on their friends, encourage them and make sure they are up to the task in place. They are usually inclined to offer you a shoulder at any point of your difficulty. Some may even help you prepare so that you are in a good mood to take up your challenge. The digital world has made these follow-ups easier since an individual may just text or email to find out what is going on other people's lives.

The best people in life are those who push you to achieve your goals. These kinds of people usually focus on them rather than the negative. They are usually inclined to think that your failure will be their failure too. This is the drive that makes it easier to always make follow-ups and impact on their friend's life. At some point this may take a toll on your inner emotions if you are the type of person can fall prey to envy. Take a scenario whereby you have been in an endless search for a particular job with no fruits whatsoever. Then your friends get this particular type of job. It is important to know how to react to situations like those. We are all human and we face challenges. When you start feeling envious, it is advisable that you channel your feelings towards something productive. For instance adopting a school of thought that if your friend has acquired that job, you are going to gain more knowledge that will be of aid to you next time you are applying for the job

Communication has always been a key aspect of any relationship. Failing to communicate properly or adequately in a relationship usually takes a toll on the relationship itself. This is because some actions of the adverse party may not be justified. For instance when you feel like you are in a relationship and you are not being appreciated, it is important to channel these feelings towards informing the other party. Let him or she know what you don't like. Address issues as they come and never let a past dispute ruin your relationship. Talk to each other and make sure that you have resolved a matter before moving forward. With regards to emotional intelligence, it is both an innate and a learned characteristic which means that you can still achieve it.

The Impact of Emotional Intelligence on Friendship

As human beings, we are often inclined to make friendships. These types of relationships are what keeps us going all through the hard times. Friends are usually a source of joy in your life. They tend to be there for you in times of need because they are aware that you would not forsake them when they are in the same shoes. In order to maintain this kind of relationships, one needs to understand the value of their friends and never look back. With regards to personal life, different people react to different stimuli in a different manner, this refers to the fact that we are not all the same and thus understanding the nature of your step is a bold move towards maintaining that relationship for ages. Personal relationships vary in broad categories. There are some relationships that need to be nurtured and followed through adequately whereas there are others that maintain with even minimal communication between the two parties.

In a relationship, the impact of emotional intelligence will always be seen in times of trouble. The effects of emotional intelligence in a relationship are:

Feeling of pity towards another in times of pain

When you are in a relationship, you are there to support your partner in times of need. You are inclined to do everything necessary in order to make your partner feel better again. Owing to this fact, you will not be in good books with yourself if your friend is undergoing emotional torture and you cannot be of any aid. The art of being aware of what your friend is going through and putting everything aside in order to make them feel better again is what makes the difference in a relationship. Lowering your emotions down to where your friend's is and having a feel of what they are going through is the first bold step towards a healthy relationship. In a relationship, people feel loved when you empathize with them no matter how worse the situation might be.

Being able to engage in a crucial conversation without emotions

A higher emotional intelligence keeps your agenda to the core and prevents you from falling away from it. Engaging in meaningful conversations I what sustains the relationship. Communication has always been a key aspect of maintaining proper relationships. You need not hide the fire inside you and let it consume you form the inside. Letting it out is one bold move that ensures you let go of all the toxic feelings. A critic is someone who will tell you the truth no matter how bitter it may seem. Criticism sometimes may not be welcomed because it tends to escalate feelings and bring about friction. The fact that we are not perfect as human beings make us learn from our mistakes. For instance when you are in a personal relationship with someone, and the status of their hygiene is wanting, it is better you address the issue as it is rather than suppressing it and letting it burn you for as long as you are in that relationship.

Expose your Vulnerability

Opening up to the other partner is one way of maintaining the relationship. As human beings, we are all vulnerable to something and that is what makes us human, we have imperfections that we carry with us all the days of our lives. Talking to your partner about this helps build your self-confidence and also builds the confidence of the other party in you. When you express your fears to the other party, they feel valued and appreciated. They also feel like you believe in them and thus they would not let you down. For instance an individual may be having a problem with smelly feet, this may be as a result of a fungal infection or biological disorder. Sharing this with your friend helps build your self-confidence, it also allows your friend to try and help you in any way that they can.

An apologetic mindset

In a relationship, especially a personal relationship, mistakes are bound to happen. You are bound to make a number of mistakes. However, how we get back on our feet is what determines the continuity of the relationship. It is good to realize and acknowledge your mistakes as part of making everything right with your partner. It is not always a walk in the park to own up to your mistakes and take remedial measures. For instance, you had forgotten that your partner gets irritated with a particular type of cologne that you wear. When you realize that you are in a mistake, emotional intelligence seeks that you make amends as early as possible and make sure that the same kind of situation does not recur. Here you need to make a point of talking to your partner about it. Make a point of saying sorry until you are certain that they are okay.

The easier flow of feelings

With an emotional intelligence in place, you are inclined to talk about the truth and not get hurt with the truth because that is what makes us better, Keeping quiet about a particular aspect does not help at all. Some individual tends to use silence as a signal that they are not happy in the relationship. Normally this sign is usually met with many questions and if not careful that may be the end of your relationship. Lack of emotional intelligence will see an individual not communicate his or her feelings. Failure to express your feelings will not be of aid in making you feel better. For instance here is a friend who is not happy with his or her partners' drinking habits. The friend has a phobia of communicating to the friend about this issue because they fear it might be a wrap to the existing relationship. It is important to communicate because if not the drinking habit it will wrap up the relationship.

CHAPTER 8
Impact of emotional intelligence on social life

In life, there are many factors that will make an individual bold. We as human beings go through various challenges due to the desire to achieve. Life is usually a bumpy road, one that is full of critic, neglect and even abuse. In order to be able to get hold of all these factors, an individual needs to learn to master how to carry out themselves on the face of these kinds of challenges. When relating to other people, one needs to understand that it is not only their emotions that is at stake. Human psychology can be subtle to comprehend and thus an individual requires to be apt emotionally in order to be able to conquer.

In life, emotional intelligence becomes evident in how we manage situations and come up to solutions on impending problems. Emotional intelligence is usually rated by how well an individual responds to different kinds of pressure and stimuli. The response to this kind of situations will help you to detect if a person is completely emotionally intelligent or he or she is not. Comprehension of others emotions is as subtle as it may seem. In order for one to achieve this, you need to be in control of your own emotions first. A deep comprehension of one's emotions helps see himself or herself in others. Putting yourself in other's shoes will ensure flow of emotions.

A higher emotional intelligence will always see you making the right decisions that may ensue positive impacts in your life. Some of the various impacts that emotional intelligence encompasses include:

Making your Career

At the workplace, what sets the pace for you is normally your colleague or even the boss. Comprehending your position at the workplace and sticking to it is one bold step towards achieving. Emotional intelligence at a workplace, for instance, helps individuals relate with one another without crossing boundaries. It helps an individual discover his or her role in the workplace. Understanding your role at the workplace helps you to stick to the instructions of the boss and avoid friction with him at any point. This in place, you have an environment that is favorable to you and in turn you are favorable to it. At the workplace you void more friction with other staff. You own up to your mistakes and make amends as early as possible rather than adopting a cover-up kind of nature. Research has it that people with high emotional intelligence usually have a top-notch performance at their places of work. Although it is normal to find an individual with high emotional intelligence not being a top performer. Emotional intelligence is in direct correlation with financial earnings. Research has it that emotionally apt people tend to amerce more wealth than less emotionally intelligent people. The nexus between financial earnings and emotional intelligence is often so direct that an increase in one variable often leads to an increase in the other.

For instance, when you are at a workplace, there are a number of factors that may test your emotional intelligence, take a scenario whereby one of your colleagues has lost a close relative. An emotionally intelligent mind requires that one should empathize with others. You as an individual need to make an effort of relating to the believed at personal level and letting them know that you care about them. This, in turn, brings about cohesion at the workplace. Cohesion brings about performance because as the old adage goes two minds are better than one.

Life-Saving

Emotionally intelligent people adopt a let go kind of perception towards harsh emotions and feelings. When an individual realizes that he or she is bigger than the emotions and problems at hand, they are able to respond positively towards such emotions and thus get relief of the same equally faster. Holding on to emotions, in turn, takes a toll on oneself. Clinging on to past experiences that were not in your favor will always keep the fire inside you burning. Having a continuous fire burning inside you will eventually consume you. Failure to employ emotional intelligence as a way of managing your emotions, in turn, makes an individual focus on other methods of managing emotions. These other methods are usually less effective or short term in nature. Their effect will only last a while and after that and individual will rescind back to his or her normal behavior. The only way of having a hold of your emotions and making sure that they do not turn you into a slave is making sure that you are apt emotionally in order to be emotionally intelligent. Moreover, research has it that most emotionally intelligent people tend to suffer from illnesses.

Illness such as depression is as a result of the accumulation of your past experiences and not letting them go. Depression at its onset may not be felt and rather would be detected in the later stages of development. When the mind is curtailed by such factors such as depression and stress, concentration shifts and settles with these factors. The ability of the body to fight impending diseases is also curtailed. As a result, the individual likelihood of falling prey to sickness is enhanced. With this in place, your body will be attacked by various diseases. Take a scenario where an individual's mind has been affected by stress, the individual is obliged to have various episodes of building castles recuperating from this stress. This individual might also be obliged to forego meals because their priorities have been reconsidered. The body requires food and water in order to continue functioning properly. Some nutrients found in food are very essential in the sense that they act as an aid to combatting diseases.

Research has it that being in distress can be linked to low levels of emotional intelligence. Various diseases such as cancer have been associated with distress and thus it is important to know how to deal with our emotions effectively. The good news is that emotional intelligence can be developed in a person through constant teaching and monitoring. Individuals who have taken it upon themselves to acquire these emotional skills during their period of illness have always been seen to recover faster and get back on their feet. Heart-related ailments are also a factor to consider because according to how we perceive information will either escalate or minimize our heartbeat.

A combination of both

Everybody's desire in this life is to lead a healthy life and also to have a career as a source of income. However, achieving both is an uphill task in that you have to apt at every juncture in your life. Emotional intelligence ensures that you balance both your mind and body. This is because at your place of work you tend to focus mostly with your brain and once your brain is exhausted, you need to take rest or engage in recreational activities in order to rejuvenate your mind. The body will maintain its health through what you ingest. You need to take note of what you put in your mouth because the development of your mind also depends on the same. Research has it that there is certain number of foods that improve the health your mind and body whereas there are others that tend to affect your body.

For instance taking of nuts, leafy vegetable and Omega 3 found in fish product enhances the body's immunity to fight diseases. Omega-three for instance is a component that improves brain growth. Emotional intelligence helps an individual balance both a clean mind and a clean body. A clear mind is important to an individual's performance at work. When your mind is devoid of all the factors that make it depressed, your concentration levels increase. An increase in your concentration levels enhances your performance at the place of work. When your performance at the place of work is top-notch, you tend to move through promotions with ease. A clean body reduces chances of distraction at the place of work since you have no peculiar smell, an aching stomach or a worn outback. This means that you are at the top of your game and thus you are able to achieve more.

Persuasiveness

This is the art of influencing others who are not in your shoes to think like they are in your shoes and in turn adopt your own school of thought as theirs. The art of persuasion involves influencing others to make them buy your enthusiasm. In order to be persuasive enough, one needs to play about with the emotions in the context. Normally people will feel convinced when they relate to a particular scenario. In order to be persuasive enough, you need to move with the currents in the emotions. Once you are out of context, people will tend not to be swayed by your idea. Emotional intelligence helps an individual to know when to introduce a subject and when to let go. You may have not persuaded somebody but the impact you have created in their minds is immense.

Take for instance, at all junctures of life a person needs to be emotionally intelligent in order to know what to communicate. You cannot attend a funeral laughing and applauding the same way you may not attend a wedding yelling at the top of your lungs sorrows. This means that in order to be emotionally in context you need to be emotionally aware of the impending factors. Your mind works best when you're aware the factors before you engage in any conversation.

CHAPTER 9
Define emotional intelligence

The main kind of intelligence known to man basically is mental intelligence. This kind of intelligence refers to making decisions, understanding and also comprehending things. For centuries man has tried to understand and dig deep on the spectrum of mental intelligence. He has looked at how it has evolved over the years, how it evolves in a person, ways to test mental intelligence in a person and also the ranking of mental intelligence. Man, on the other hand, does not just have this one side to him he also has an emotional side to him.

Does this emotional side of man carry its own intelligence? That brings me to emotional intelligence. I know you are asking yourself are emotions governed by one's intelligence or they have their own guide? To give an answer to that question I will just define what emotional intelligence is. Therefore, emotional intelligence refers to the ability of a person to feel, relate and express his or her emotions. It seems bizarre that how these controlled by intelligence rather than a response. The explanation is very simple stating that emotions are both a response and are also connected to the intelligence too.

The reason why emotions are both based on intelligence and response is this, one always knows how to react to a certain situation that is clearly, response.

It usually feels like a natural switch to how one reacts. Emotions too are intelligence since one needs to know and measure how they react just like learning how to cook like a fine example. This concept may seem confusing but it is easy to remember one is inbuilt while the other is something acquired over time. They are both important in understanding how human emotions work at all times.

Emotional intelligence helps us understand so much of a person. This may be how he or she is feeling and even knowing their opinion about something. One is born with emotions same as the mental intelligence but the emotional intelligence has to be grown or expounded. It acts like the mental intelligence which is learnt or grown in the course of time. One should practice and know which emotion is right for which occasion. To understand more of emotional intelligence one has to work greatly at understanding the general emotions that already exist in every human being that can be expressed.

To know about one's emotions then one has to know and understand themselves. Everyone is different meaning that even their emotions and their emotional responses are different. Some people are stone-hearted while some people are so light-hearted. One has to first understand themselves then the rest will be easy. Emotions are expressed differently in people. The way you and I express our joy or sadness is different but it is very normal. It calls to show that we are very different and unique. The more one gets this then even get the concept of emotions will be very easy.

Another thing that helps in better understanding of emotional intelligence is motivation. Motivation is the ability of one to go for something because they have a driving force. Motivation is a part of emotions there are theories of motivation and how they work. The most important thing about motivation is the fact it goes together with the everyday living of human beings. One must have self-drive to know themselves. That brings me back to self-awareness which is a key factor to emotional response and also intelligence. There is so much more to motivation like what it entails and even its typed too.

All in all emotional intelligence is something inborn in everyone. It has to be nurtured from a small age. This is to allow a child's emotions to grow with no hindrance. This is a subject that should not be taken lightly. The more someone is able to express their emotions then the easier it gets to interact with other people. Interactions involve social skills which are channeled together with emotions in a conversation or any kind of interaction with others. This then shows us the importance of emotions and their understanding of human life as an aspect to it.

CHAPTER 10
Define emotional intelligence appraisal

Since most people take tests to know their mental intelligence they can also do the same with their emotional intelligence. This is what brings us back to emotional intelligence appraisal. Emotional intelligence appraisal refers to the way in which people can measure one's emotional intelligence. It is also a series of questions just like in mental intelligent test. They are very sophisticated to cover all aspects of man and all his emotions. Some people even believe that they surpass the normal intelligence quotient test given to man. The emotional intelligence test is not that popular.

The test is set psychologically to fit the emotional needs and answers of man. Emotions are connected to behavior hence these test helps to identify certain behaviors on certain people or men. Behaviors are different in men and so are emotions. The emotions quotient is also graded as the intelligence quotient. The test helps to rank people in different bars of their emotional ability. Some are good at having their emotions in check while others are really terrible at it. Hence, it brings the similarity of both the intelligence quotient and the emotional quotient. It helps in racking intelligence on each of the sides.

The emotional intelligence appraisal is the test to know how someone will get which job and how they will perform in it and lastly also how they will relate with others. Emotions determine a very big chunk of people lives. They are in communication and also decision making among other things. How one is emotionally wise shows where best they can fit. Like calm people who can deal with drama and are good listeners are mainly judges. Their coolness and calmness in the face of judgment make them the perfect fit for being in that position.

Emotional intelligence appraisal is said to have some components in it. One of this component is how one can manage his or her relationship with others. Between self and people who are closest to the person, there must be mutual understanding. One must understand one's behaviors and flaws and even the good things that come with him or even her. Behaviors are clearly a very big thing that is matched with emotions since they are their biggest trigger. If one does not get used to someone's behavior especially if they are close then that close relationship is bound to fail.

The other component is learning to manage oneself. This may mean so many things but in this case, it means controlling one's emotions. This means knowing what to say or do at the right time and with the right people. This to avoid offending people with their own behaviors. One must be cautious of what they say and do. Learn to be better at controlling one's feelings and emotions too. Understand that others are human and that they are important too. This helps in keeping one in check of all their deeds and actions towards themselves and also to others.

It is also good to know and understand oneself is important. It helps to understand your certain unique behavior. You are also able to understand how you react in different circumstances whether good or bad. In the end you teach yourself in the right emotional responses. It is more of hard work since when you get to understand yourself then others become easy to interpret while interacting with them. One learns on the arts of taming oneself in the things you do worst and enhancing what you do best. The saying I might use in this case is you do you.

The last aspect or component is understanding or knowing others. This clearly seen or done after one has understood others. After understanding self then it is easier to know about others. Emotions not only affect one as a person but it comes in and affects all the people around this person. Knowing others and how their emotional response is thus very crucial. The more one understands others the better their relationship is which makes living with others very easy. Clashing with others then is very easy to avoid if you just are willing to give a chance to others.

Emotional intelligence has proved to be important as mental intelligence. It has been seen to guide people's every day to day lives from work to school and homes too. It has shown the importance of the relationship. Also self-awareness has been touched on for some part. Socializing with other people has also been seen as key in the world of emotions. The emotional intelligence appraisal work was to give ranking also give and opinion of how someone's life ought to be because of their emotions. The more one understood this then one could work on fixing his or her future.

CHAPTER 11
Different ei test methods

Emotional intelligence is measured through self-report and others report as well as through others report. Self-report is used when one wants to evaluate themselves. Through a self-report, one is able to evaluate their personal traits and be able to give honest feedback about themselves. This helps them to be able to work on their shortcomings and also improve on their strengths.

Others report about us is also very crucial. It is in order to seek peoples opinion about us so why not? The people around us have different opinions about us. They know our capability to handle emotions since they have seen us react to different issues at our place of work and even at home. However, different people will give a different report about us. Some will be honest with u while those who are not sure about our behavior will give inaccurate reports about us.

An effective emotional intelligence test will be able to analyze our self-report, others report and through others report and be able to come up with one report about an individual. This is the only way to ensure its accuracy. The emotional intelligence report is tested through different methods which are listed below.

The Emotional Quotient Inventory

An emotional quotient is a tool which is used for the purpose of evaluation of one's emotional and social functionality. This is a tool that gives a clear report about someone's emotions and also how to fit they are when it comes to socializing. An emotionally intelligent person is defined as one who is able to handle every day's challenges successfully. They handle all the pressures around them and manage them effectively. This is a tool that people can use to measure their emotional strength and weaknesses since one can be able to tell the areas that need improvement and those that they are strong in. this is because the tool gives feedback that is very valuable.

One does not need to worry when the test gives bad feedback. This is because emotional intelligence is said to develop over time. They are skills that can be nurtured through as well as improved as time goes by. There are people who are aggressive enough to grow these skills by themselves. These are people who take everything positively. It means that they are able to identify the areas that they are weak in and work on bettering them. There are others who take their time and have to be coached in order for them to acquire emotional intelligence. This only means that they are slow in acquiring them but they will eventually acquire the skills.

Emotional quotient inventory is a tool that measures so many areas and in different settings. It is normally incorporated in the corporate world, in the medical field and also in other research settings. Research states that the EQ-I tool is very effective when used in a business setting. This is because leaders can use it in the management of their emotions. They will be able to make improvements in the way they communicate with their employees. The employees will be able to do their best in their given field. They will also be able to communicate with their employers whenever they are faced with any kinds of challenges. This will in return bring sobriety in the working place which will be helpful in the delivery of services to the clients.

Some leaders are said to use this EQ-I tool when hiring new personnel. They have supplemented the evaluation tool with the emotional intelligence tool. This is because the intelligence tool is more accurate. Every employer should work on employing emotionally intelligent people. It will mean that the employees are emotionally stable hence can handle all kinds of pressure on the company. Every employee will be able to make the changes in the company positively and will work towards efficiency in everything that they do. A company can also work on nurturing employees with emotional intelligence problems. This will be for the good of the company since their skills will be used for the growth of the company. An emotionally intelligent person will be able to go the extra mile to ensure that everything is handled efficiently.

Profile of Emotional Competence

Profile of emotional competence is referred to as a tool which was thoroughly researched for the purpose of measuring intrapersonal emotional intelligence as well as one's interpersonal emotional intelligence. Intrapersonal emotional intelligence is all about knowing all the good things about yourself and even all the bad and ugly things about yourself. By knowing everything about yourself, you will be able to control your emotions whenever you feel like there is a need to.

Interpersonal emotional intelligence is defined as the ability to relate well with the people around you and being able to communicate with them effectively. Through interpersonal intelligence one may be able to coach the people around them on ways of managing their emotions especially the people that one feels like they have the same temperaments as you. You will be able to easily coach them through the methods you used for you to manage your emotions.

It is a tool that has become very popular over the last two decades. This is as a result of their effectiveness and efficiency of its results. The public and the scientists have diverted all their attention to the profile of emotional competence as a result of the popularity that comes with it. It is through a profile of emotional competence that many people have been able to learn about their emotions and ability to control them without relapsing.

Research has been continually carried out which has been said to assess all the parts of emotional intelligence which include identification of emotions, understanding emotions, regulation as well as how we use emotions. Through the research, individuals have been able to learn that being weak emotionally is not the end of them. There is something that they can do about it. There are also other people out there with the same emotional problems as them.

Profile of emotional competence is normally used for evaluations of one's emotional intelligence as well as that of the people around you. However, it cannot be used when hiring or even for compensation. This is because it is a tool that is continuously used since it assesses people's emotions at different times and days. Profile of emotional intelligence gives a thorough report about someone. This is because it is able to analyze how everyone feels as well as how they feel about the people around them.

This tool normally used as it is proven to have results that are consistent. Its results do not have a really big difference so they can be relied on. As a result of the profile of emotional competence, researchers have come up with different models which include, knowledge and abilities as well as traits. The knowledge level is used to assess people's knowledge of emotions. There are people out there who may not have any knowledge about themselves. They may not be aware that their poor emotional management skills. This test will enable them to be able to discover such things.

The abilities level is used to assess people's performance which may also mean their capability. Abilities level is also used when assessing people's ability to apply the learned knowledge and how they apply it to real-life situations. The trait level is used when assessing one's ability to hold it up even in situations that are extremely emotional. This trait becomes a success when one can consistently deal with their emotions efficiently in emotional situations.

Profile of emotional competence is said to have given effective results as compared to all other emotional intelligence tools. It has been able to measure different areas of emotional intelligence effectively which has enabled people to be able to understand their emotions in a better way. People are also able to understand the emotions of others. This has helped them to be able to understand them better and in return being able to deal with them even with their varied emotions. Nothing feels better than being able to interact with people around you despite them having different emotional intelligence. It makes everyone's work easy since they do not have to struggle to interact with the people around them.

The trait of Emotional Intelligence Questionnaire

The trait of emotional intelligence questionnaire is referred to as the instrument which is used to measure the universal trait emotive intelligence. It was developed by K.V. Petrides when conducting their scientific research in London. The instruments used when conducting a trait emotional intelligence questionnaires are normally free and anyone in the clinical or academic field is able to easily access them.

These questionnaires are normally available in different languages so people from different parts of the world are able to get access to them in their most preferred language.

When using this tool, one is able to find out if they have the ability to manage their emotions even as they interact with people with different emotional intelligence. It is a tool that is very crucial when carrying out research on emotional intelligence. People and especially those in the business world are able to deal with the complex situations they face in their day to day activities. This is because they understand their strengths and weaknesses perfectly. They have knowledge and skills that enable them to deal with different pressures each day.

It is a tool that helps employees to be able to discover themselves, their ability to develop meaningful relationships and even how adaptable they are when it comes to handling situations at work. The trait of the emotional tool is also said to be helpful in the improvement of how employees engage one another at work and also how much loyal they are to one another. Most employers tend to use it since it has been proven to be the best research intelligent tool with instant proven results.

The trait of emotional intelligence questionnaire has been proven to work best when detecting anxiety and depression in people. Through the questionnaire, whether the long form or the short form, one is able to derive information from the given answers. This is a tool that is of great benefit since those affected will be able to look for help early enough.

The trait of emotional intelligence questionnaire normally exist in long forms and also n short forms. There is also a trait questionnaire for children which is made in such a way that it examines children related domains. It is used in children aged between eight and twelve years.

The long-form questionnaire contains reports totaling to 153 on self-report which uses 15 subscales. It is a questionnaire that takes utmost 15 minutes to complete. A short-form trait of emotional intelligence 30 questionnaires which use a 7 point scale for all the items and also takes a few minutes to complete as compared to the long forms. This is a tool that has been proven to work efficiently as well as in a reliable manner. All its results are said to be valid hence the need for people to consider using it.

Wong's Emotional Intelligence Scale

Wong's emotional intelligence scale is referred to as a self-report emotional intelligence which is based on different abilities. It is used in the appraisal and expression of one's emotions, ability to recognize other people's emotions, ability to recognize self-emotions and ability to use your emotions to expedite emotions. Wong's emotional intelligence is said to be successful when an individual is able to control their emotions as well as recognize the emotions of others whether sad or happy. It is also termed as successful when one is able to handle situations at work or even at home without being overcome by emotions. Being in a position to handle one's emotions efficiently makes Wong's emotional intelligence scale successful. This tool is also used when one wants to measure trait emotional intelligence. It is a tool that has been proven to be very reliable and accurate. Many researchers worldwide have therefore turned to use this tool which has also made it very popular worldwide.

CHAPTER 12
Define (eq)

Emotional Quotient

Emotional quotient is the measure of and individual's ability to reason accurately, but with a focus on emotions, and uses the motion and knowledge about the emotions to improve himself in terms of thought and action. Mostly, emotional quotient focuses on the emotions and the reasoning that brings about emotions or guides them and uses them to improve one's thought. It brings out the intelligence that one has and joins it to emotions observed to see how much thought can be improved. Emotional quotient is gotten by relating given set of abilities that relate in complexity, ranging from the one that requires less skill to process such as the perception of emotions, to complex skills that require understanding, differentiating and managing emotions, or even generating new emotions. These led to four branches that are involved in the determination of emotional quotient. These four branches are systematic in nature and are as follows: perception of emotions, using emotions, identifying emotions and managing them. This system is systematic in a way that one cannot have the highest skill, which managing the emotions if he or she does not have the ones that require simple skills.

Emotional quotient is not measured generally because emotions are different and they are also processed differently, therefore, when dealing with emotional quotient, the procedure of obtaining it is done in a way that there is specifying of emotions, called the specific of emotions. The recognition of positive emotions such as being happy is totally different from negative emotions such as feeling sad. These emotions also have different effects on an individual and also managed differently. Therefore, emotional quotient uses two approaches to bring out the ability of an individual in terms of perceiving, using, identifying, and managing emotions.

They are a specific-ability and the integrative approach models. In the specific ability, a particular skill is considered important in emotional intelligence and therefore included in the emotional quotient. Some models that take this approach assume that some emotions can facilitate think while others cannot. For example, when one is angry about a service, he or she was offered, the emotion can trigger that person to start a business that would offer better services. This will be a different case for a person who has experienced happiness with the same service. In this case, the negative emotion led to a good decision that would bring about better services, but the feeling of happiness did not facilitate anything. This means that even negative emotions are good and can bring out positive aspects of life. Positive emotions can also bring out something good, for instance a frustrated innovator might fail more times than a happy innovator. This is because a happy innovator creates an environment that promotes creativity in his or her mind while a frustrated innovator drives away creativity. Therefore, a model can choose an emotion that would bring out good result, whether negative or positive and include it in the emotional quotient test.

Other models that take up the specific-ability model concentrates on the individual's understanding and emotional reasoning. These models assume that any emotion brought about by a situation, and certain emotions are only triggered in a particular set of situations. For example, a person who is seen to have fear must be facing a life-threatening situation, which affects his thoughts, and consequently brings out a fearful emotion.

Other models might choose to look at emotional self-management. This might include looking at situations, and instead of flowing with the thought that things will continue to get worse you reframe yourself to think otherwise. In this case, the person has changed his or her perception, thus controlling himself or herself. The model would choose an emotion that brings out a characteristic that is desirable and includes it in the emotional quotient.

The second approach to emotional quotient involves choosing different abilities and combining out a better emotional quotient that is representative. This approach assumes that the chosen abilities grow together, even it if not at the same rate; there is no way one can be skilled and be poor in the other and yet they are related. These tests are usually meant to eliminate the faking of abilities. The approach takes into account the four branches of emotional intelligence. One cannot manage emotions if he or she does not know the emotions he or she is managing. For instance, you cannot be empathetic when you do not aware of the feeling of other people. The skills, therefore, are assumed to grow simultaneously and emotional quotient score is high when the two are related in a positive way.

Some psychologists also came up with another approach besides integrative and specific-ability approaches: Mixed model approach. This approach does not only focus on emotions but also include other characteristics such as the need for achievement, flexibility, self-awareness, and assertiveness, among others. This addition makes the definition of emotional quotient to include words or phrases that do not show emotions, for example, competency, non-cognitive or skilled. In most cases, the emotions and non-emotion characteristics complement each other. For instance, a socially competent individual easily controls his anger, and a stress-tolerant person is happy than a stressed person.

Goleman on the hand came up with another approach. He argued that everyone is born with the potential to improve his or her emotional quotient by gaining emotional knowledge (competencies). The competencies are therefore learned and can be improved and worked to get high emotion quotient scores. This model, therefore, basis its quotient on one's experience. An example of such a model is an appraisal which looks at the quotient level of the person using items or questions that relate to his working environment. The competencies include social awareness, which involves sensing and reacting to other's emotions. Self-awareness, the reading your own emotions, and self-management, which deals with the control of own emotions and adjust to new situation. Managing relationships, which is the ability to develop and influence others

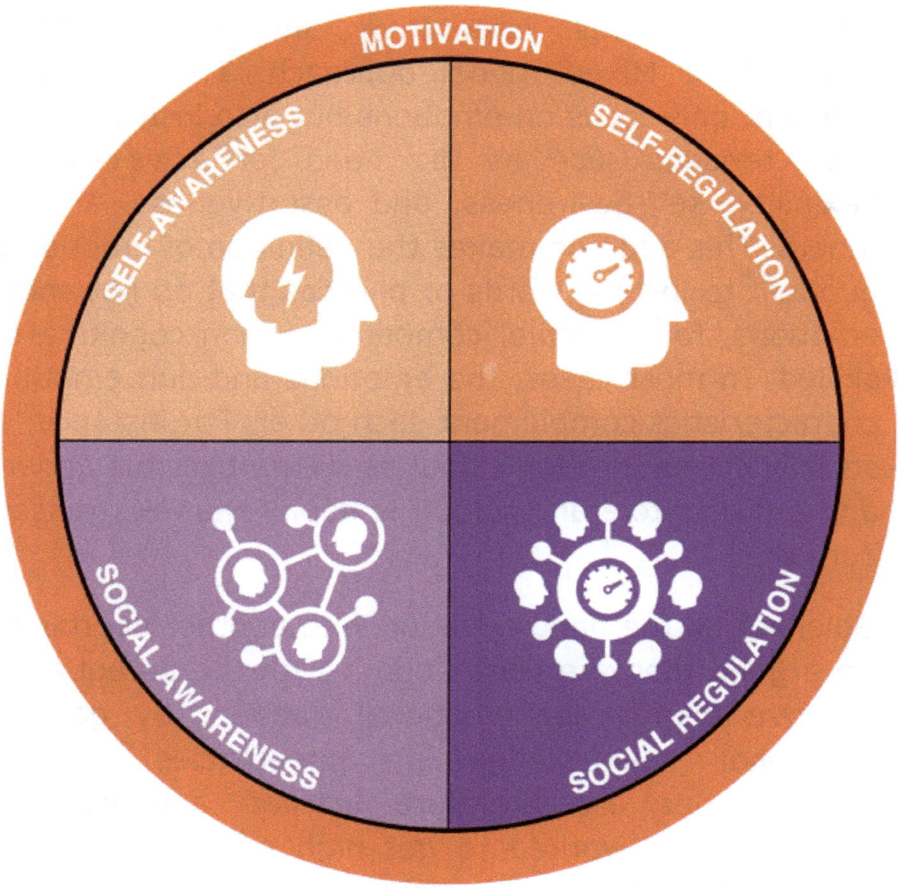

CHAPTER 13
The 6 eq tests

The MSCEIT

The MSCEIT quotient test is an EQ test that assesses using the ability-based scale. The scale is used to measures an individual's performance of tasks and at the same time solves emotional problems. This test assumes that the skills shown by an individual are developed as the person advances in age or matures. These skills can be improved through training of an individual for a given period. The score in this test is usually not affected by the emotional state of a person, set of responses to the questions provided, and self-concept. The MSCEIT is a test that is in line with the four model branch that deals with emotional intelligence that is arranged systematically as accurate perception of emotions, good use of the perceived emotions, being creative in solving problems, understand emotions and manage them for personal growth.

In the four model branch, the ability of an individual to perceive emotions is measured using faces and paintings. An individual is presented with a picture showing and asked to indicate the emotion displayed on a scale of five. When using pictures, an individual is asked to judge the picture by looking at the landscape the aspect of the use of emotions is measured using the facilitation and sensations provided by the individual.

An individual is asked to imagine the presence of certain emotions and the different situation in which they can be applied. In the case of facilitation, an individual is asked to give an extent to which emotions can be helpful to someone in a given situation. For example, an individual is asked to explain how fear can help a hunter.

The aspect of understanding of emotions is measured using the changing of emotions and blending of emotions. In blending, an individual is asked to give a situation where basic emotions combine to result in a more complex emotion. On the other hand, in changes, an individual is asked to give a change that might occur if certain feelings or emotions are intensified.

The ability to manage emotion to your advantage is measured through emotional management and having a good emotional relationship. In emotional management, an individual is asked how certain actions can regulate emotions such as being happy and sad. In evaluating emotional quotient, each aspect is given a score and an overall score gives the emotional quotient.

The Schutte Self-Report Emotional intelligence test (SSEIT)

This test also uses the four branch model of perception of emotions, using them, understanding, and managing of emotions. The SSEIT test is structured to look like the branch of MSCEIT, with 33 questions whose answers give a report on individual a scale of 1-5, where 1 mean strongly agree while five means strongly disagree. Just like in the MSCEIT, each set of questions is graded and added to give an overall grade that gives the emotional quotient.

Bar-On EQ-i

The Bar-On EQ-I test was originally designed to analyze the emotional concept and social functioning of individuals. It is used as a self-assessment tool to measure an individual has a socially acceptable behavior. This test measures empathy, interpersonal effectiveness, impulse control, assertiveness, reality testing, and social responsibility. This test consists of 133 items, which takes between 30 and 40 minutes. The test uses the five-point Likert scale with one representing "very seldom" and five represents "very often". The Bar-On EQ-I is not suitable for children, and therefore only people who are 17 years and above use it. The total score of the test is usually accompanied by 5 EQ composite scales that have 15 subscales. The composite scales include the general interpersonal EQ, mood EQ, stress management EQ, adaptability EQ, and intrapersonal EQ. these scales give a total score that is used in the analysis that gives an average score that shows whether a person is emotionally healthy or emotionally intelligent. A higher score in the section is used to predict a generally good score in the whole test, which gives the EQ of an individual.

Trait Emotional Intelligence Questionnaire

Trait emotional intelligence consists of emotional perceptions of an individual that are assessed through rating scales and questionnaires. This test concentrates on people's beliefs concerning their emotions. The first questionnaire was developed in 1998, and it contained items that covered facets such as emotion regulation, stress management, self-esteem, impulse control, assertiveness, emotion perception, social awareness, trait empath, optimism, emotional expressions, and self-motivation. This facet of traits and many others add up to 15. The questionnaire that is in use today contains 153 items that cover 15 facets of traits, global traits, and the other four factors. This test has received a lot of negative feedbacks but is still considered by people who want to test how a person operates in a given physical environment or deals with changes in emotions of other people or even their emotional changes. It has been considered as the test that brings to light the personality of a person, although it is considered to be at a lower level compared to other tests for personality. It is the most used emotional quotient tool in today's world, especially for screening candidates competing for leadership posts. It is also used to predict behavior in children to predict their behavior when left under certain circumstances.

When conducting the tests, each question has no fixed answer, and the individual answering the question is at liberty to express themselves either in wring or oral.

The answer is then evaluated depending on what the one who is conducting the test is looking for. For example, when an item is looking for high self-esteem, an individual will be asked questions that bring out the self-perception; is it strong or not. The emotional quotient is determined by the score of items in different facets and the total score is the EQ of the individual.

Emotional and Social Competency Inventory

This is an EQ test that concentrates on emotional competencies postulated by Goleman. Most of the time, it is used to help an individual improve or work on their competencies. The test measures 18 competencies, but they are all put in four clusters: relationship management, social awareness, self-management, and self-awareness. Self-management involves an individual's ability to control impulses, internal states, and resources. This cluster contains six competencies: optimism, achievement, initiative, adaptability, self-control, and transparency. The cluster of self-awareness involves one's preferences, internal states, intuitions, and resources, and contains competencies such as accurate self-assessment to know what are your limits and strength. Other clusters include self-confidence and emotional awareness. Relationship management desirable responses to others; this cluster contains competencies such as conflict management, teamwork, influence, developing and inspiring others. Social awareness involves handling relationships, being aware of other people's concerns, needs, and feelings.

This cluster contains competencies such as service orientation, organizational awareness, and empathy. To calculate the EQ, each competency in each cluster is given a score and from the scores, an overall score for each cluster is obtained and added to get the final score. It is the final score that gives the EQ of an individual.

Situational Test of Emotional Understanding STEU and Situational Test of Emotional Management

These two tests for emotional quotient are new. STEM and STEU wants to deal with the last two branches of emotional intelligence. This model refers to the first two branches as the experimental stage and the last two are the strategic emotional intelligence. The STEU and STEM are therefore considered as the highest level of emotional intelligence, with STEU taking the understanding of emotions part while STEM takes the highest branch of managing emotions. The STEM, which is the highest branch and more complex achieves a high personal and interpersonal growth and at the same time includes cognitive, emotional, and motivational factors.

STEU measure of emotional quotient involves looking at the ability of the person to connect emotions and events, which follows a framework theory that says that specific reactions are caused by specific events that bring about emotional responses. STEU has 42 scenarios with emotions such as anger, frustrations, stress, hope, sadness, contempt, surprise, and dislike, among others. The scenarios contain items with multiple choices, 14 of them are reduced, 14 of workplace context, and 14 have personal context. An individual is given these items and asked to describe emotions that are presented in each context. A score is either a correct answer or incorrect. This makes it different from other emotional quotient tests.

STEM, on the other hand, measures the ability to come when under stressful situations through the regulation of negative emotions and promoting the positive ones. The items in STEM are semi-structured and the answers are given by choosing between the options. The test has 44scenarios with three specific emotions: sadness, anger, and fear. The emotional state is described in each scenario and four possibilities provided on how to solve the scenario. The participant should choose the best option, and who chooses the best score

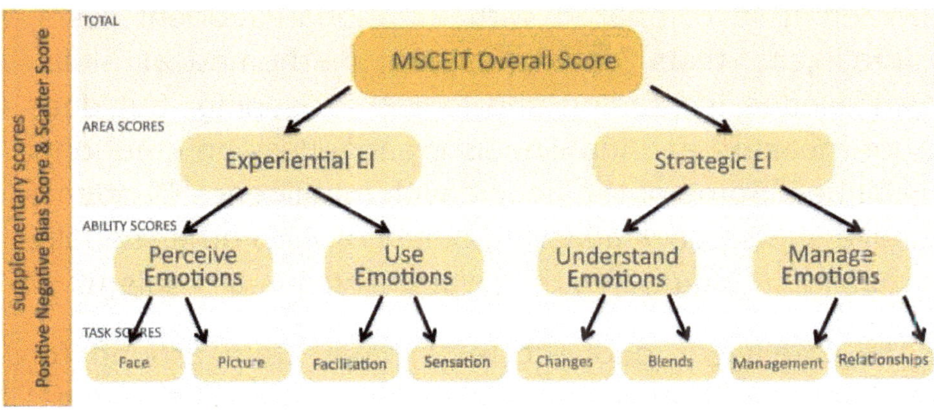

CHAPTER 14
Is emotional quotient test equals to intelligence test?

Emotional quotient is not equal to intelligence quotient because a person with a high intelligence quotient might have high emotional intelligence and vice versa. The two quotients are equally important for they contribute to the success of any human. However, emotional quotient test can be used to measure the ability of an individual to succeed in life, and that is why most of the time it is tied to the level of success most successful people. The brain theory stipulates that a person with high emotional intelligence has self-awareness and confidence; there he or she can easily navigate through to achieve success as opposed to the one with high intelligence quotient.

When it is compared with emotional quotient tests, intelligent tests only measure mathematical skills, knowledge in reading and logical reasoning, but does not measure and individuals creativeness on emotional abilities. Some of the people with intelligence Quotients have shown poor adapting behavior with other people, thus maintaining healthy relationships is a problem.

The intelligent quotient tests have been around for quite some time when they are compared to emotional intelligence quotient tests, which developed later. Again, looking at their use, emotional intelligence quotient tests are done more friendly in workplaces than intelligence quotient tests. This because intelligence quotient tests they only test how the person can do the test but no how the person can relate and operate in an environment with dynamic situations. Remember that most employers would like to see results in action and not on paper; therefore they prefer emotional quotient tests to intelligent quotient tests.

Emotional intelligence quotient can also increase significantly with time, as a person gains experience and becomes competent in the emotional and social aspects. This is not the case with intelligence quotient because an everyday interaction does not expose one to much work that requires word problems or logical statement. For emotional quotient test, everyone interacts and faces different situations, there is growth, and there is a possibility that the nest emotional quotient test one is likely to be a notch higher than in the previous test.

The intelligence quotient tests only involve the testing of the cognitive aspect of a human being while emotional quotients tests involve emotional, social, and cognitive. In the emotional quotient test, we talked of the four branches used in measuring emotional intelligence and the most complex branch requires a lot of thinking, same to what is involved in the intelligence quotient test. Therefore, using an emotional quotient test has an additional value.

The end result of an intelligence quotient test is the person is able to think in the abstract, and if this is looked at critically, does it have many benefits to a person living in a highly socialized world. You bet it is not, but emotional intelligence quotient test has. Going through several emotional quotient tests would help one to perceive emotions, use them effectively to their advantage, and learn how to identify different emotions and how to manage them to better their situation.

The intelligence quotient tests are aimed at an individual and how his mind works. This means that it is in isolation with other factors that shape his or her life. The person is therefore considered an "island", which he or she is not. This is not the case for emotional quotient tests, especially those used in appraisals; they are work-related and a person gets feedback that is useful and not frustrations. In addition, these tests are sometimes difficult, making those who undertake them to feel that they are not better people. There is also likely that whatever is being tested in the intelligence quotient tests is not related to the work one is expected to do, and therefore not affect in choosing the right candidate for the work, or unfair judgment of those who take part in the tests.

Looking at emotional intelligence quotient tests, the scores to the tests are arranged in an order of from the least to the highest for each item and others allow free expression of the participant. This can show a progressive improvement, something that is not seen in intelligent quotient test. The intelligence tests have fixed answers, for instance, the correct pattern is always one, and a logical statement is also one. Such a test does not help one to grow.

Intelligent quotient does not keep in mind all aspects that make up a human being such as attitude, culture, dreams, economic background, and even level of education, as well as a level of exposure, and there, they are not fair in judging who has high intelligence and who do not have. The emotional intelligence quotient to an extent incorporates these aspects, as it deals with interaction with people and how emotions play a role during the interactions and how better we can improve. Therefore, the judgment made at the end of the tests is valid to some extent.

CHAPTER 15
Emotional intelligence exercises and activities

Emotional intelligence exercises and activities are endeavours to improve and develop personal emotional intelligence, understand the emotions of our team in group and to build our social skills as an individual or team leader. Emotional intelligence (also referred to as EI) exercises and activities are basic to anyone who wants to succeed at a personal level or at a leadership level. For those who want to better in their leadership role, understanding your own emotions is the most important step then you will find it easy understand your participant's emotions.

In modern society, a large number of people are yarning to improve their EI and for different reasons in each case. Below are some of the reasons for wanting to build our EI.

- Succeeding in the leadership role.
- Understanding our own personalities.
- Knowing the people around us better.
- Enabling ourselves to adapt to a different environment.
- Learning about different traits in others.
- Sometimes accepting different situations as they come.

In most cases, EI for many people is always important in enhancing leadership skills. They tend to forget that they also need EI for personal growth. People are born differently and with different character traits. This is why we can't always have the same emotions and it becomes hectic understand other people's feelings.

There are several EI activities and exercise that help us individually and as a group. As a leader, you will find yourself at some point questioning why some things just have to happen, and why always you. In this article, you are going to learn the EI exercises and activities that will help you as a leader and also as any other person.

Reasons most people turn out as "bad" leaders are because;

- They tend to treat others badly.
- They have a tendency to command everyone.
- They always want other people to do as they say.
- They never accept correction.
- They think they are always right and others are wrong.

In a team the some important EI activities include;

Having Great Vision

As a team leader, you must have a vision for whatever you are doing. Always ask these questions;

- Why do we have this group?
- What do we want to achieve?
- Couldn't I do it myself?
- Do I belong here?
- What is my role in this particular task?

These 5 questions will help you understand better why you are involved in a particular activity and you will be motivated to work hard towards achieving the goal that you for the sake of empowering others. As a leader, you will find it, even more, easier to work with this team because you already know what you want to achieve and probably have some idea on how to go about it. You will realize you not alone and you are not going to strain in order to achieve this particular goal. Having the same vision with your team is the best way to go.

Sharing Your Vision

Letting your team know your vision is a good move. Let them know how you feel, what you have in mind and what you think is better for the entire team. By sharing your vision, the participants in your group will get to know more about you and what you have in store for them. Sharing your views with them will have some influence on them and in most cases, you will always find support from your team if you have an effective vision. It is important to make your team aware of your vision as their leader.

Asking for Other People's Views

As a leader, you should know that not everyone in your team knows what they want. It is always very important to ask for everyone's view so that you get to know what exactly they have in mind. You should not be the one to make a decision for them. In most cases, you will find others having the same view which will sometimes differ from your own. Do not take any offence when you have different views. The best you can do is to have both of you explain why you think particular is important and why you should go for it. This will help you arrived at the same junction.

Working towards the Vision

Usually, after you and your team have come up with the same vision, the next step becomes working towards that vision. Work together as a team on how you are going to achieve this vision, know what you have at hand, what you need, and how you are going to use what you have to get what you need. Joining hands to work together as a team makes your efforts more successful than doing everything alone, so have your team involved in every single step.

Seeking Advice

No one is perfect. It is healthy to seek advice from professionals to get better ideas on how to achieve your vision. There are those who are experienced in the field of your line. Ask them they did it, what led to their success. Look for the experienced team leader and have them advise you on how you need to work with your team. It is true there are different ways of killing a rat, but collecting ideas is also important in coming up with a different and unique tackle.

Picturing Yourself

You had a vision as a team leader. You shared your vision, gathered other people's views and got advice from different people. Now sit back and picture yourself. Are your views on the same line with your team? If not, did you get along with them? Did you all agree with the same thing? The advice you got from other team leaders, are you able to practice them? Are you ready to try something new? Once you have everything in order, then you are good to go.

Reflecting on the Vision

Take time to rethink on your vision and mirror it. Is this what you want? Are you in a position to achieve it? Scratch your head and look into it, see if you made the right choice and be sure that you don't really need to change anything.

Taking Action on the Vision

Up to this far, you already know what you want, you have your feelings in order and those of your team. You now have to take action, make a move. Do whatever it is you have to do to achieve this vision. Concentrate on the successor activities to your vision. What should be done must be done and what is not productive should be avoided.

The exercises of Emotional Intelligence include;

Assessing Your Emotional Intelligence

Know your own emotions and know how to deal with them. As a leader, understanding your individual emotions will help know how to deal with them around anyone. Learn the emotions of your participants. This will help know how to approach them at any moment and you will be in a position to balance each person's feelings.

Showing Passion

Develop passion in what you are doing and let your team know that you are passionate about them. It will be easier dealing with everyone if you have the passion to work with them. You will do everything without a feeling that you are being pushed or that you are doing it for anyone. You will work as if you are working for yourself and everything will move smoothly.

Concentrating on the 'Whys'

Try finding out why ideas vary from person to person, why you have different ideas with your team and why they think you are wrong and they are written or why you think you are the one on the right and not them. When you understand this, you will always be ready to face every situation without finding an offence.

CHAPTER 16
Using ei tools

Being emotionally intelligent will improve your performance in the office and everywhere. Everyone around you will love to see you carry out everything with intelligence. There are several EI tools that you can use to enhance your social skills and those of people around you. Understanding people is never easy, but these tools will help you widely in this field and you will always love yourself for who you have become a person, as a worker, as an employer, as a leader or a parent.

Everyone wants to be understood and treated right. Nothing feels better than knowing that you have a positive influence on those who look up to you. Basically, no one ever wakes up in the morning and find themselves intelligent, neither is anyone born intelligent. There must be an influence in your life that will make you grow emotionally and feel valued. To be more exposed in the field of EI you have to research deeply and allow yourself to adapt the changes.

Educationists have much focused on the EI tools that are helpful to society. This is because we all need to learn. People interact differently and with different people. We meet stranger occasionally in our day-to-day's activities. We come across people with different emotional influence but in the end, we find ourselves getting used to them and adapting to the changes in the new environment. What all of us need to know is that you can never understand anyone's emotions without understanding your own. Neither can you change anyone's mentality without showing them an acceptable character?

By the end of this chapter, you will be pleased with yourself because you will be a different person. You will have learned the different EI tips and how they influence other people's lives.

The most popular EI tool is Personal Emotional Intelligence Awareness. Everyone is in charge of their own emotions. Being aware of your own emotions is a great step. This is the only way you can get to learn how to interact with people from different environments. You can only be of good influence to others when you are in a position to understand your feelings and manage your emotions around them. Learning other people's emotions also becomes easy and you can easily fit in their position without offending anyone or being offended.

You can visit sites that talk widely about emotional intelligence. These sites contain comprehensive information which is modified to help you learn easily and absorb the techniques that are useful to you everywhere. They increase your level of understanding and accepting changes. They also influence your attitude positively and change how you conceive things.

Creating a good working relationship with your colleagues is another tool that is more useful when it comes to working. You can only develop good working relationship with people if you are the type that accepts instead of being personal with everything. Learn to accept your mistakes and correct them. When you make a mistake and you have to be corrected, accept, change and move on. Also correct others when they make mistakes without holding any offence.

Don't be the dramatic one. Avoid to your level best-causing drama around people. Being dramatic lowers your integrity as a person. Everyone is human and they make mistakes. Controlling your emotions will always keep you out of trouble. Don't just be that person who attacks everything head-on making situations worst all the time.

Never be judgmental. Judging only means you don't take time to understand the people around you. You may be depressing someone's emotions without knowing. If you read deeply into EI tutorials, you will learn that understanding people's emotional states is also part of improving your social skills.

Another important tool of EI is self-motivation. Always keep your mind positive that everything is possible and believe in what you can achieve. Learn to appreciate yourself for what you have achieved and keep aiming higher. This will change your mind about everything and keep going.

Empathy is a tool of EI that involves observing others, understand how they feel and trying to fit in their position. By emphasizing with others, you help them come out of their sad situations without making them feel unwanted or unfit in society. You help them notice their value and ability in life.

Applying these tips in your every day's life will help you in mental and social development. It allows you to accept your environment and also enables you to fit in all kinds of environment. EI tools also help you to understand others and support them mentally and emotionally. As a parent, it helps understand your child's emotions. You get to know their fear in life and you be in a position to offer them emotional assistance.

CHAPTER 17
Eq worksheet examples

Creating an EQ worksheet will help you know exactly how emotionally intelligent you are.

1. Use of Quizzes and Questions

Using the quiz and tests with a score will help you analyze exactly where you are and highlight areas you need to improve so that you increase your EQ. The quiz should cover;

- Your ability to understand and assess your strengths, weaknesses and personality.
- Your ability to identify, understand and manage your emotions.
- Facts about emotional intelligence and self-awareness.

On top of giving you an outline of your emotional intelligence, it will also help you practice skills such as;

Information recall - you will be able to access the knowledge gained about emotional intelligence and self-awareness.

How to interpret data - when you go through your test, you will begin to understand and identify what the scores and answers you gave mean about how you view yourself and the people around you.

An example of an emotional intelligence worksheet below:

Data	Quiz	Honest Answer	How you intend to improve on it. Specific. Eg, rather than 'to communicate better', say 'to begin to take a keen interest in others
Self-Regard	How do you view yourself? How confident are you in your abilities? How do you view your		

	opinions? Do you see them as better than other peoples?		
Emotional Self-Awareness	What is your state of emotions for most days? (generally sad? Angry? What leads to such a state of being?		
Emotional Expression	How do you express your emotions? Are the ways constructive?		
Impulse Control	How do you react to sudden stimuli? Why do you react in that manner? Do you often think through		

	the consequences of your impulse reaction? If you do, and still go through, what informs your decision?		
Interpersonal Communication	Do other people seem to enjoy being in your company? Why do you think they like you? If they seem to not like you, how does that make you feel? Do you feel satisfied with how you express your feelings and opinions with		

	others?		
Empathy	Does the emotional state of another person have an impact on you? Does injustice make you angry? Does someone else's grief leave you sad? Are you able to understand someone's actions, even though you don't agree with them?		
Social Responsibility	How do you view the world around you? Do you feel a sense of responsibility		

	to improve it? Do you feel a sense of responsibility with how you relate to it?		
Problem-Solving skills	How do you manage conflict? In your anger, confusion, guilt, do you listen to others?		
Reality testing	How does the world affect you? Are you grounded in reality, or do you tend to live in your bubble?		
Flexibility	Are you able to change your opinion		

	in the face of compelling evidence contradicting your widely held belief? Are you open to accommodating others' shortcomings? Do you question your opinions and beliefs? Are you open to learning?		
Stress Tolerance	What stresses you the most? When you hit the melting point, do you still manage to remain engaged and logical, or do you panic? How do you		

	avoid finding yourself burdened by your stress?		
Optimism	Do you view the world favorably or unfavorably? What shapes your view? How does this affect your actions? How does this affect how you relate to other people?		

2. The Open Door Policy

This project is divided into three parts; Knowing Yourself, Choosing yourself and giving yourself.

You could then, put it down on paper, with each sheet containing the part you will address, staring with 'Knowing Myself', then 'Choosing Myself' and finally 'Giving Myself'.

Knowing Yourself

Knowing yourself gives you an insight into your strengths and weaknesses. You will gain an insight into what shapes your actions and what you want to be the result of those actions. Write down the 'what' you want.

Choosing yourself

This provides the 'how' you will take the actions to get what you want. This creates intentionality behind your actions. Rather than reacting, you do what you choose and mean to do. You become proactive.

Give Yourself

This details the 'why'. Why you pursue the things you do and why you respond in the way you do. These help you put your 'how' into action.

While on the face of it, this seems selfish, being in touch with the core of who you are, makes you more aware of the world and builds your empathy. Because you know the struggles you go through, you then sympathize with other people going through their own problems and become more willing to share your insight with them to help them. So, try the above methods and all the best.

CHAPTER 18
Ei programmers and workshops

Some countless programs and workshops will help you in improving your emotional intelligence.

The Daniels Goleman Emotional Intelligence Coaching and Training Programs

This program is often geared towards improving a sense of personal agency and a positive impact on oneself and others.

It is often a hands-on learning experience, with the learner required to partake in exercises that would help you gain a deeper understanding of not just what emotional intelligence entails but also, how it applies to our daily lives in real-time. The program includes a virtual course and a coaching certificate.

Once you are through the training program, one can also choose to pursue the Daniel Goleman Emotional Intelligence Coaching Certificate, which is designed for those who are interested in coaching others in EI.

Through this program, there is the Individual EI Coaching model, which emphasizes three key elements;

Learn: This has practical explanations and examples of EI, delivered as an article or a video. This is aimed at developing your proficiency in the Foundational and Relationship skills of EI.

Apply: This is an immediate application of what you have learnt in each lesson which then provides you with insights that will become essential in your daily life application, be it in school, at home or work.

Reflect and journal: this is aimed at helping you maintain your self-awareness, which is described as 'the cornerstone of this model'. Having a daily journal helps create an archive for your mindset and how you think. This will allow both you and your coach spot counterproductive habits of the mind and pinpoint practical strategies to work with your specific challenges.

Institute for Health and Human Potential (IHHP)

This institution offers training on your terms, and have a variety of training programs in their line-up.

Their virtual training facilitated their delivery of the Science and Emotional intelligence programs which then allowed their clients the flexibility to get training in the schedule that works best for them.

These EI programs drive real behavior change by providing participants with the knowledge and tools to manage their emotional brain and the most difficult moments in their life.

The fact that they tailor-make their training to fit the participants' terms also means that you will likely learn a lot from this, as their programs aim to address the needs of the organization. This helps especially when it is difficult to find the time and resources to leave work and go to the workshops.

The Emotional Intelligence Institute

Like the Daniels Goleman program, this institute is specifically dedicated to developing emotional intelligence. Through workshops and masterclasses, they can improve the EI of the people that go to them, be it employees, supervisors and managers.

It is based in Perth, Australia but they have an online learning center, called the Tele-Classes, which has live video streams from experts, as well as online EQ seminars (webinars), all at an affordable price.

They have three series to their online EQ Tele-Classes;

The FOUNDATION Series; they are open to anyone, anywhere and are often an introduction to the essential aspects of EI, emotional resilience, job interviews, networking and presentation skills.

The SPECIALIST series; They are often specifically tailored towards the application of EI for professions and industries, for example, HR Professionals, real estate and government professionals.

The LEADERSHIP series; they are geared towards high-ranking officials, such as CEOs, CFOs, COOs, board members and other people in senior leadership positions who find themselves working as the head of a large group of people.

Lead Change Group

This is a website that offers articles by psychologists and other leading experts on how we can master, be mindful of our emotions and how to channel them to communicate effectively.

Through articles such as 'Use Emotional Intelligence to Address Speech Anxiety' or 'Effective Communication is about Understanding Emotions', they teach us how to handle and manage our emotions.

The Trust Thermometer

This is a group activity that is aimed at fostering interpersonal trust through an exercise.

This exercise involves participants to line up against a wall and step forward as they respond. Several real-life scenarios are played to the participants and they are asked to make moves according to the level of trust they think they have in each case. Conditions may include:

A friend borrowing money, a friend blindfolding you and taking you to an unknown place and having lunch with strangers. When someone doesn't make a move, it means that the person had no trust in the situation and the individual involved in it. Taking 4-5 steps would imply that a person has complete trust in the circumstances before them.

This activity doesn't need a class so it is something that can be organized in, say at the workplace or school to foster good communication between co-workers, which would then lead to gaining trust. It also helps in learning how to read a person's mood and body language and how to respond appropriately.

Genos International

They are known for developing the Genos Emotional Intelligence Model. This model aims to build EI through a set of emotionally intelligent workplace behavior competencies.

They offer the Genos Emotional Intelligence Assessments which measure how an individual displays emotionally intelligent workplace behavior that underlies success. They are usually peer-reviewed research and accompanied by reports that provide accessible and practical development suggestions.

The Genos EI Enhancement Programs

These programs transfer content, assessment, frameworks and tools into practical behavioral changes that endure and have an impact. The programs provide what they describe as 'holistic approach' to development by improving both foundational and functional skills for the modern workplace.

The use of the Genos EQ psychometric assessment helps identify candidates with high emotional intelligence in the initial screening. Candidates will then be interviewed and taken through role-playing simulations, after which there is an EI assessment to introduce them to expected behavior at the workplace. This is then followed by a confirmation to ensure the employees are demonstrating EI sufficiently in the business using a 180 or 360-degree assessment.

Alternatively, if all this seems too much, you can get in touch with one of Geno EI Model biggest trainers, Wend Jochum, from Australia. She is qualified in the Geno model and has a vast experience in human resource, learning and organizational psychology.

CHAPTER 19
5 ways you can develop emotional intelligence

Emotional intelligence allows one to be able to read the other person and respond appropriately. This helps you then build trust with others. Emotional intelligence is a skill that gets better with practice. It is more than just being an outgoing person. To be emotionally intelligent is to understand another person even in the pockets of silence. It is the ability to see, identify and correctly interpret the non-verbal cues of the other person and respond appropriately. It is being able to tell what someone is trying to communicate even when they don't say it. All this sounds easy, yet we all get it wrong most of the time.

So, how then, do you develop EI and build your charisma? How do you become more personable?

Create Self-awareness

Realistically assess yourself and come to terms with what you are capable of and how that affects how others perceive you. Self-awareness is the ability to recognize and understand your character, moods and emotions and how they affect you and the people that associate with you.

1. *Know what you are doing* - de-clutter your life so as you put focus on what matters to you. There is a rule

called the 80/20 rule, developed by Italian economist Vilfredo Pareto. The rule posits that 80% of consequences result from 20% action. Therefore, when you know what you are doing, you will be able to focus your actions on the few important things that result in the highest results.

2. *Know how you feel* - mastering your emotions is a great way of coming to terms with how healthily or unhealthily you deal with the emotions within, especially the negative feelings. This often will scare you. You will find that maybe you are someone who is pretty irrational, or very pessimistic or are often angry over little things. Do not judge yourself when you find out about them.

3. *Know the annoying triggers of your emotions* - once you become aware of your emotions, you will then follow them down to what triggers them. Then comes the second step.

Positively Channeling Your Emotions

Once you become aware of how you feel and how you react, it is then important to identify ways in which you can channel them well. A shared belief among people is that you need to control these emotions. Emotions often are a call to us to change something within, and around us.

As Mark Manson would say, "*there are no good or bad emotions- there are good and bad reactions to said emotions*."

Anger, or sadness or shame, are not bad emotions. Anger is destructive because you choose to react destructively to it. But, if say, you use it to become an activist and fight injustice, it then becomes constructive. Sadness is damaging because you react in a counterproductive way to it. But if you use it to push yourself to pursue what makes you happy, it becomes constructive. The follow up to them is what counts.

Practice Empathy

Empathy is the ability to perceive and react appropriately to how others feel. It is about understanding and sharing the feelings of another person. On paper, it seems easy, but in practice, it is a hard emotion to master.

When you develop a positive outlook towards the world, you will become more deliberate about how you relate with others. This awareness of moods will help you guard your attitude and instead, give you a chance to try and understand why the other person/people are acting the way they do.

For example, it is empathy that would allow you to know how to properly comfort someone who is feeling sad. It is what triggers the anger in you when you see and injustice. When you become someone whom other people relate to, you will develop better relationships with them. This does not mean you become tolerant of bad behavior, rather, you become aware of the fact that everyone has their issues. In a professional setting, where we spend most of our adult life, this will especially be useful in helping you relate better with your coworkers.

Communication - Mind Your Language

Becoming an effective communicator is an important part of being emotionally intelligent. The choice of words we use daily is often a reflection of how we feel and how we perceive the world around us, and consequently, how we react to it.

Emotionally intelligent people often use more specific words that can help bridge out any misunderstanding. Did you argue with your partner or a co-worker? What led to it? What did you say that triggered them? What did they say that made you act out of character?

Words often will leave a lasting impact, especially when said in a heat of the moment scenario. To build your emotional intelligence, be aware of the words you use, and how you use them. This will help you become assertive, but without being aggressive. You will communicate your opinions and needs without sounding disrespectful to others.

Active Listening

After a conversation with someone, do you find yourself hard-pressed to say what they said? Not word-for-word, but the key point of their speech?

In conversations, emotionally intelligent people tend to listen for clarity, rather than to just react to what was said. And the sad part of this is that, in many instances, people will often just be waiting for their turn to speak. Thus, they will not be invested in what is being said.

To build your EI, listen to what is being said and understand before responding. Part of this will also involve you taking in the non-verbal cues, an essential part of any conversation. Language only expresses a part of what the other person is feeling. Therefore, when you listen beyond their words, when you listen with your ears and your eyes and a conscious mind, you will respond appropriately. Plus, it will show that you respect the other person.

CHAPATER 20
8 ways of improving the emotional intelligence on the workplace, relationships

Psychology has become very diverse because it involves understanding the interpersonal and interpersonal feelings of a person. The human system is mostly comprised of three aspects, which means our physical life, spiritual life, and psychological life. The emotional aspect of a being sometimes hard comprehends. You can never predict the next behavior of a sensitive person unless you are an expert in analyzing their feelings.

Those experts are referred to as emotional intelligent persons. These people should not be confused with smart persons or bright personnel. At one time you have met a person, whom you presume to be brilliant, but their actions are questionable, you wonder what the significance of that cleverness is. Such people do not know how to express their emotions. In a simple sense, they act weirdly to people and themselves.

How the emotions are formed in the body is a difficult question to ask. Moreover, they are feelings which cannot directly be traced to their production point of the body. Some may argue that they are generated from the mind, while others may say they are conceived in the heart. If you love a fellow, then that is an inner feeling mostly attributed to the heart. Emotions are therefore typically processed in the heart and transmitted for interpretation to the brain. To know an individual who has such qualities one must first consider the components of this attribute

Components of Emotional Intelligence

Understanding your feelings is instrumental in attaining emotional intelligence. Your attitudes are dynamic and diverse, where many individuals do not deduce them accordingly. Most of the times, one can only know their reactions when being told by others. Comprehending your feelings helps one to reflect on how they affect the individuals close to you. If you are involved in a disagreement, the intelligent person will know the point to control his attitude.

Managing your emotions is always attributed when you recognize your feelings. This process requires you to know the right emotional aspect to apply in a particular scenario. It also helps one to identify the best point to express your feelings. By doing that you can combat any conflict and disagreements you have with another person. Such fellows also are credited of cooling their temper where they change quickly from a bad mood.

The third component is when these individuals accurately interpret the mood of their colleagues. That is one quality that should be found in a manager when interacting with the subordinates. Those going to strike may tell you that their leader is not able to communicate and understand their resentment. If you have high intelligence, you can observe the reaction of a person you are integrating with and anticipate his next behavioral pattern. A good psychologist can read your emotions and construe your life experiences.

Having high emotional intelligence (EQ) helps one to manage the relationship between yourself and other people. You therefore easily comprehend and interpret the reactions of other people. You are also equipped in regulating the behavior of others even in the event of disputes. Such people are always chosen as leaders or mediators. Sitting in a table with rivalling parties requires one to consider the interests of everyone at hand appropriately. The person with high EQ will justly rule the case.

How to Improve Your Emotional Intelligence

There are very diverse people with different characters. Therefore, it requires one to improve their emotional interpretation of those individuals occasionally. Psychologists have gone as far as trying to interpret emotions using science like empathetic forecasting. That is where they use statistics like measuring the correlation model between an empathetic party forecast of all people concerned. Yes, in some instance, the research work but no one can measure the behavior of a person. The following are the ways of improving your EQ.

First, you should take the correspondent inner feelings and experiences like they were yours. That means you are putting the situation of a colleague on 'your shoes.' When doing that you can clearly define what the other party if feeling. You can therefore intelligently advise them on the next step to take. By doing this the respondents feel their feelings being cared and personalized.

Be attentive in listening when the other person is speaking. Always check on their nonverbal cues and try to analyze that pattern. Try also to deduce the different emotions they show like analyzing their tonal variation and gestures. Makes sure there are no distractions while listening and acquire a mental picture of what they tell you. When they notice your keenness and interest, they will reveal all their inner feelings.

Be flexible in changing and adapting to their mood. In the event of a quarrel, intelligent people will usually mitigate violence. That is done by adjusting to their partner's point of thinking and deducing some sense in it. Therefore you can even find out you are the wrong party involved. When they are wrong, do not criticize them harshly but first, credit their thoughts and market your idea politely. Leaders, judges, and mediators should possess this character in making rulings.

Deliberate on your weak point as of the other. If you are hot-tempered when wronged, you should know how to control yourself. That is because, in conflict, you should cool down to avoid further violence. Moreover, you should be quick to detect the shortcoming of the other. The person with a good EQ can manage that person accordingly. That is because they know the criteria to handle different weakness of a person. For example, if a person has a personality disorder, you can calmly handle their grievances.

Always inquire for others for feedback and information. Emotional intelligence is like a skill that needs to be learned. Therefore you cannot obtain the knowledge by yourself .consulting others for feedback help you gain more understanding of a particular area. Moreover, their response will help one notice their reactions and sentiments. Acting on their feelings will build trust and healthy relationships.

Always be motivated to learn the behavior of other people. In this context, variable people show different feelings. Learning helps one in gaining knowledge. You will also understand how to handle various emotional aspects. You will be equipped with ways you can advise such fellows. You can also use your personal experience when meeting with people of personality disorders.

Always be optimistic about every situation. There are very various scenarios that come with their difficulties and needs one to approach them intelligently. A negative attitude harms the self-belief of a person in accomplishing some tasks. You may face such a person and sometimes it is hard to interact with such individuals. However, approaching such a situation positively gives you that motivation in understanding their sentiments.

Emotionally intelligent personnel are approachable and social to others. They are free to talk to and to intermingle. They have excellent interpersonal and intrapersonal skills. They are self-aware of their conscious and do not like to engage in conflicts. They can relate to any people and are skilled in articulating their values to them. In the process of interacting, they learn the emotional patterns of many people and use that information in dealing with those victims.

6 WAYS TO know a person is emotionally intelligent

They are usually curious about other people. Ever interacted with police or an investigator? What about the questions they asked you, were they many? That is what these people are. They always want to get at the bottom of every piece of information. They are curious about your mood change and why such changes occur. Your information about an absolute scenario helps them to learn and understand your emotional state.

They are quick to embrace change. This aspect means the experts are flexible and diverse. When arguing with them, you will find out that they easily let you win the argument. That means they quickly adapt to your ideas. Tailoring to your thoughts is always a wise decision that is fair to all parties.

They stand by their point in most of the times. Such people are assertive and cannot be convinced otherwise. They are always principled and try to articulate the valid values amid a conversation. These experts know how to express their views while ascertaining their beliefs courteously. Therefore by doing this, they command respect from their colleagues.

These fellows can convince people in a more considerable aspect. That is where they articulate their ideas to the opinions of another. That is to say, and they are persuasive of the things required to do. They usually conceive your attitudes, feelings, and values and connect them to what they want you to do. Their polite and understanding treatments are some convincing elements they apply.

You will waste a lot of time if you want to offend them. That is because they are hard to get angrier. They are ever jovial and social. Whenever you dispute with them, they will navigate ways to escape the disagreement. They may even let you win that disputes at the expense of their welfare. However, they will intelligently connect their preferences into yours and make you see their significance.

They possess effective communication styles. They are very proficient in the language they speak, which is engrossed with vocabularies and fluency. By this, they command respect from the correspondent where they earn trust and confidence from those colleagues. They possess excellent listening abilities because they attentively listen to a speaker. Every word including the non-verbal cues is vital them particularly. Turn-taking and serious talking are other virtues associated with these people.

CHAPTER 21: A 3-4 weeks plan on how to test and improve our emotional intelligence on workplace relationships

WEEK 1: MANAGEMENT OF NEGATIVE EMOTIONS

Most of the times, there are qualities that you may seem to hate in a person. These characteristics are mostly their ill behavior. Consequently, in our daily lives, people experience bad moods and attitude. These aspects are mainly facilitated when one is wronged, or unexpected events or experiences occur. Such situations prompt victims to show negative emotions.

These emotions are hurtful to people you relate. For example, a wife may suffer from the anger and insults of the husband. These negative behaviors are the vices in the society as they result in adverse effects. Such effects may lead to committing of murder, domestic violence, and many other illicit actions. It is, therefore, upon you to control the wrong emotions so that you cannot find yourself on the wrong side. If one has to learn how to manage them, one has to know the following causes as listed below.

Societal background and teachings are some of the causes. The highest percentage of what one believes is influenced by the parents or society as a whole. Some of the vices are even inherited from guardians. They say that 'like father like son' therefore if your mentor possesses an unpleasant attitude, you are likely to inherit that emotion. Sometimes the societal teaching shapes one in whom they are.

Experiences of depraved events and situations may make one adopt negative emotions. If particular persons wronged you in the past, you would be angry with them at all cost. Whenever you pass through a painful episode, it leaves you a negative stigma engrossed with awful feelings. Therefore this results to you to blame others for your misfortunes and to be pessimistic on a particular subject.

Comparing yourself to others makes one angrier if the other colleague is better in some ways. People have to understand that people are gifted differently. Therefore, do not compare yourselves with others. In this case, you will underestimate your abilities and believe for others are perfect. That is the genesis of low self-esteem. Think of how low self-esteem persons behave because they usually are angry, envious spiteful, fearful, and hateful.

Putting your desires, in front of others, causes a negative attitude. That is where you feel you have to compete with other fellows, and you adopt a jealous approach if they succeed. You are always gluttonous in wanting to have everything at your disposal. You feel rage when others do not treat you as expected. You still want to show some pride so that others can recognize you.

Ways to Manage Negative Attitude

First, you ought to identify the negative emotion that you possess. It may be that others say you are greedy, temperate, or pride. In particular areas, there are attitudes where only your colleagues can tell you. Do not be afraid to ask even your close friends what they sometimes hate in you. You may be thinking things are going well, whereas some of your behaviors are unpleasant. Reflect on a time you caused some chaos, what did you participate in that disputes. When you know the terrible attitude you have, you can reflect on how to change it.

You can meditate on the effect of that emotion. There may be a time when you were fully raged, and you assaulted someone. Therefore the relationship with that person broke. Or you lost your best friends because you were proud to focus on your interests than theirs. When you realize the terrible impact of that behavior, you will brainstorm on the best ways to change. Always choose to reconcile with the colleague you wronged and inquire how they expect you to behave next time.

Deliberate on the source of that attitude or disdainful character. You cannot fight something which you do not know where it originated. It is always right to think about the cause of the vice critically. You may be surprised to realize that the reason is something you never expected. Take an example of a person who is arrogant because he is the number one swimmer. Hey, there is no wrong of being a number one swimmer; however, overstating your success is wrong. Therefore for that scenario, you have to be calm and appreciate your challenges.

By reading or sharing your resentments with other people helps one to manage a particular ordeal. You may think that you are the only one who has a personality disorder but also others do. Make a point of sharing with others on how they resolved their evil characters. You may be surprised to know that what you are passing through is less than what they are experiencing. Read journals or browse on the internet to understand how to cope with such a situation. Allow your close friends or relatives to correct your actions. In the process, they will advise on the best way to manage the emotion.

Improving your feelings is another way to mitigate unwarranted attitudes. It is not a matter of how to eliminate your distress, but a matter of how you can improve the ill emotions accordingly. For example, one may be suffering from fear and anxiety, but you can manage them. If you are shy in public address, then practice talking to a small group, and with the time you will improve in this area. Engage other friends or psychologists who can recommend you better ways to improve your behavior.

Control your attitude effectively. After learning your mood and knowing that effect, this is the best point to learn how to control. If one is temperamental, you have to learn how to cool yourself on every occasion. If possible, set the control techniques and write them down. You can even tell a person to alarm you when you have that emotion. With time you will monitor yourself and try to regulate a situation once you feel the behavior is approaching. You will develop this habit, and with time, it will end.

Look for the right company. If you stay around people, who has a negative emotion as there is no way you are going to change. However, if you hang around with mentors and emotional intelligent guys, you will absorb their character. Soon that unwanted attitude will come to an end. Through this socialization, one can inquire their approval on every action you take. If they are satisfied, know that you are in the right progress.

CHAPTER 22
A 3-4 weeks plan on how to test and improve our emotional intelligence on workplace relationships

WEEK 2: MINDFUL VOCABULARY

Mindful vocabulary means paying close attention to the way you use your words as you communicate with others. It entails choosing your words carefully to avoid hurting others while expressing your emotions and feeling. This is what someone means in professional and social circles when you hear them tell you to mind your language. Mindful speech is a product of EQ, or what is called EI, standing for emotional intelligence. Words have power, and mastering to use the right words can make or break relationships. Being mindful with your vocabulary can bring you success at work and in your day to day interactions. Mindful speech is not easy, but you can master it with practice. It is worth the effort because the benefits of learning to choose the right words depending on the situations are huge. The kind of words you choose can determine whether you are honest, harsh or mindful of others.

Refrain from harsh speech

Words have the potential to harm. The impact which harsh words leave on us can last for a long time. Using rude and angry speech makes you act violently towards others. Most of the time, when we are mad with our colleagues, we tend to use words which are intended to inflict pain on them. Speaking when you are angry can make your words get out control, and end up saying things which are not even right in the first place.

When you feel the impulse to speak out of anger, it is good to hold back your words and stop the conversation for a moment. This will give you time to cool so that you can resume the discussion with control, and speak clearly with respect. You will then have avoided the trouble of letting your words go viral and inflict pain on your friends, and the embarrassment which comes later on when you cool down. When you are harsh in your speech, your colleagues and friends will avoid you.

Choose the right words at the appropriate time.

Different types of speech have their appropriate time. The words you use to express yourself in professional situations will be different from those you use when talking casually in casual conversations. It can be very embarrassing to confuse the two environments. Using words casually can be uncomfortable in work-related professional situations.

Your friends will feel humiliated and embarrassed when you make a snide comment about them at work, but take it with ease when discussing personal matters either verbally or on social media. While it is vital to say things as they are, knowing the right time to say what you want to say is critical in mastering how to use words mindfully. However much you may want to air your grievances or make comments on something, first consider whether the situation is appropriate. Learning to speak appropriately improves your relationship with others.

Avoid useless words

Don't talk just for the sake of it, so that others can feel your presence. You end up using words which are unrelated or unnecessary in the conversation. This can be embarrassing, and you may find other staring at you wondering whether you have gone out of your mind. Useless speech makes others be overwhelmed with you, and they may not appreciate your presence. When you find that you are talking and your colleagues are keeping themselves busy on their phones and laptops, then it is a signal that what you are saying is useless and your words do not make sense.

When you are in a conversation, consider whether the words you are using are useful and whether they will add any value to what others have said. When your colleagues at work or your friends come to realize that your words are helpful, they will pay attention when you speak and have a fantastic relationship with you.

Avoid exaggerations

Using exaggerating vocabulary makes you a liar by omission. When you exaggerate, it means that you are not speaking the truth. People exaggerate so that they can look better, to convince or to avoid trouble. This may range from the way we pad our resumes or trying to take credit where it is not due. You may feel that such little lies are healthy, but with time, they grow into a habit of lying. The way you use your words will make your friends know whether you are lying or you are telling the truth. This may get to the point where your words cannot be trusted.

When people can rely on the words you speak, you are safe. It is crucial to practice to say what is right. It will help if you learn to watch your mind and notice any time you want to exaggerate and refrain from it. Exaggeration will make your colleagues stop trusting what you say, and this may impact your relationship negatively.

Avoid slandering words

Slandering words only serve to divide. In professional circles, it is known as office gossip. When you get into the behavior of talking about others when they are not present to defend themselves, the chances are high that you are using slandering words. Slandering words are used to talk trash about others, without them having an opportunity to defend themselves. Gossip is addicting, and when you get used to it, your conversations will always turn to it. Gossip involves the use of malicious and toxic words, and the purpose of such words is only to divide, especially when they come to the notice of the other person. Therefore, avoiding slander will help you improve your relationships with colleagues at work and your relationships.

Use kind words

Being kind with your words will have a positive impact on your relationships with colleagues and friends. When you choose kind words, it shows that you are respectful and mind about others. Kindness will also help you refrain using words ignorantly and take responsibility for what you say.

Think before you speak

In a nutshell mindful vocabulary enables you to learn to consider your words, hence cultivating deep awareness on what you say. It is good to reflect on what you are about to say, and the effect it will have on others. When you feel compelled to speak, analyze whether the words you are about to say are valid, useful, kind or appropriate. It is improved emotional intelligence that helps avoid, hold back, and choose words to have a feel for others.

CHAPTER 23
A 3-4 weeks plan on how to test and improve our emotional intelligence on the workplace relationships

WEEK 3: PRACTICE EMPATHY

Empathy is one of the critical elements of emotional intelligence. It is an essential relational and leadership skill either at workplaces or social situations. Empathy allows us to put ourselves in others peoples' shoes, mind them, and understand how they feel and why their feelings, make them take a particular action or say things that they say. For you to nature a great workplace and social relationship, you need to know how to practice empathy. Empathy should be practice in three dimensions so that it can result in a good workplace and social connection.

Cognitive empathy

Cognitive empathy entails the ability to understand how people might be thinking or feeling. This can be used by those in leadership, such as managers to understand the feelings of their team members and establish the best way to get the most out of them. Salespeople use cognitive empathy to gauge the moods of their customers and decide the effective tone in which to set the conversation.

Emotional empathy

Entails the ability so share other peoples' feelings and understand them deeply. Emotional empathy affects you when you know the other person's feelings and makes you want to create a genuine rapport with them. It makes you feel immersed in the other persons' problem and feel their pain. Team leaders can benefit immensely by developing some level of emotional empathy. It helps them to build trust with their team members by developing trust and openness.

Compassionate empathy

This is the ultimate form of empathy. It involves showing concern for other people, sharing their emotional pain, and taking practical steps to help them lessen the pain. Therefore, this is an active form of empathy. Imagine a situation where your colleague goofs while making a presentation before board members. To show empathy, you can begin by acknowledging their pain, identifying with their grief by showing some of the feelings which they have and taking concrete actions to help them by showing them how to avoid the same mistakes in future.

At first, you may find it hard to show empathy to your colleagues and friends. You may fear to commit yourself emotionally, and feel reluctant to do so, but this can be practiced and yield enormous benefits for you.

Acknowledge other peoples' perspectives.

To practice empathy with effect, you need to be able to hold back your views and opinions and see things from your colleague's perspective. When you place too much attention to your own beliefs, assumptions, views, and ideas, you leave no room for you to empathize with others. It is good to approach others with an open mind and an empathizing attitude. The moment you understand, why others stick to theirs believes the way they do; you can acknowledge them. This is not to mean that you agree with their views, but it helps you to avoid arguments, disputes, and unnecessary debate. You can show respect to their beliefs and keep listening to them. To do this, you need to be emotionally intelligent, to recognize behavior that appears to be emotional, unreasonable, and

stubborn. This will enable you to know the best way to react to your colleagues based on your knowledge and experience with them hence promoting a good relationship.

Give full attention to your colleagues.

Listen carefully so that you can understand what your colleagues are trying to tell you. Use your gut instincts, eyes, and ears to get every detail out of the conversation. Take note of the keywords and phrases in the words they repeatedly use to understand their concern. Notice their tone of voice and body language to understand the feelings they are trying to communicate. Notice whether they are getting angry, feel ashamed, or scared. Go further and listen emphatically, by avoiding to ask direct questions or arguing with what they are saying in your mind. Don't dispute the facts they are putting them forth while they talk. Approach the conversation with the flexibility to notice a change in the direction of your colleague's thoughts and feelings. Keep the noise of your thoughts and feelings down while the other person is still talking. This will enable you to get every detail of the conversation, and your colleagues will love you due to the attention you give.

If you need some details to be clarified, you can ask the right questions, to get clearly how the other person thinks about the best way to resolve the issue at hand. Asking the right questions is the easiest way to understand other people.

Take some action to help a colleague.

Doing something's to help your colleague achieve some goals is a good way to show empathy; taking action will be compassion in action. When taking action, you should always remember that empathy is not about what you want, but what the other person wants. Your effort should be tailored to benefit them. If your colleague at work is struggling to do something, and they reach out for your help, do not decline. Lend a helping hand and let them learn and benefit from your skills and expertise.

Smile and show interest in others

Approaching your colleagues with a smile and taking the struggle to remember their name is a great way to show that you care for them. This makes you approachable, and they can seek out for you quickly when they need assistance.

Offer constructive feedback

Get back with positive feedback to your colleagues when they enquire something from you in a way that cares for their interests and feelings. Going silent without a response with be arrogant and will make them feel band, especially if they know that you are in a position to help them with the issues they have.

Don't use your position to crush others.

When some people rise to positions of power, they use that as a weapon against their colleagues, especially their juniors, to crush them. This is the case when they differ in opinion with them or when they fail to yield to their self-fish demands. Show empathy to your juniors by being kind to them and motivating them to achieve the desired results.

CHAPTER 24
A 3 weeks plan on how to test and improve our emotional intelligence

WEEK 4: UNDERSTAND YOUR STRESSOR AND BOUNCE FROM ADVERSITY

Improving the emotional intelligence of a person can be described as resurgence experience. People have seen the benefits of improving emotional intelligence in the current generation. It has sparked the urge to improve this critical part of human life. The concept helps a person to label, comprehend and control emotions. The most irritable question in peoples mind is commonly where they start from. A developed work plan for three weeks will prove to b of immeasurable help.

Therefore; this is the process for twenty-one days;

Day 1: Asking and Reflecting

The first day a person is supposed to create time and ask him or herself a set of questions. The questions are supposed to cut across how his or her mood affects the decision making the process, description of his or her communication style, traits in other people that bother him or her, if he or she finds it difficult to admit when wrong and his or her strengths and weaknesses.

1. Day 2: Using Of Emotional Vocabulary

An individual is supposed to try to use specific words to describe every kind of feeling he or she gets. A good analogy can be derived from the hospital environment. A doctor is will ask a patient to try and describe what he or she is feeling. He will try to use specific words so as to get to the root cause of the ailment. Similarly, when a person is able to get a clear description of what he feels, he or she can get to the root cause of unwanted emotion. It improves emotional intelligence because people can easily diffuse the problem.

2. Day 3: Pausing

This is the day a person is encouraged to pause when handling an emotional situation. One supposed to train him or herself to take walks for five minutes to ponder on his or her decisions. It gives a person the ability to calm down and regain oneself.

3. Day 4: Using the Third Second Trick

It is a critical step in implementing to improve a person's emotional intelligence. This day a person is supposed to ask him or herself three questions within three seconds before making a decision and he or she regret latter. These questions include if there is need for speaking some words, if those words are supposed to be said by him and if the same words are supposed to be said that time.

4. **Day 5: Volume Adjustment**

The fifth day focuses on a person's tonal variation while communicating with other people. One is advised to speak in a calm tone across the day because rational voice always leads to rational response. It surprises various people how calmness can be able to calm hot situations.

5. **Day 6: Thinking Over Topics To Be Addressed**

An individual has to think over touchy topics with the aim of having a rational conversation. This day a person is supposed to also know how to reintroduce heated topics. The best way it is done is by acknowledging other people's thoughts.

6. **Day 7: Fast Forwarding**

It is very common for emotions to cloud a person's judgment. The seventh day focuses on an individual thinking about the long term and short term effect of the action he or she decides to do. The process improves a person's clarity levels in life situations.

7. **Day 8: Learning From Negative Emotions**

The stage takes person footsteps back in life. He or she is supposed to take note of the lessons from his past emotional break downs. The process helps him or her to get motivated through every unwanted emotional situation.

8. Day 9: Learning From Emotional Hijacks

Emotional highjack can be described as a situation when people lose control of their emotions. The situation is mostly caused by over-accumulation of unwanted emotions. The ninth day an individual is supposed to look at what can make him or she lose control and what can he or she do if these situations are to happen.

9. Day 10. Learning To Say No

It is a great quality of learning to help other people. However, this amazing life attribute is supposed to have its own limits. A person can be at the risk of burning out when he or she always says yes to every task. A person is supposed to put his or her interest first on this day.

10. Day 11. Asking For feedbacks

People are very scared to get an honest answer to their behaviors. An individual is supposed to be courageous and go ahead to ask people about how they think of their character.

11. Day 12: Learning To Turn Critic To Constructive Response

The results from the previous day form a strong basis of this day. A person is supposed to put aside what he or she feels about the responses and work hard on the areas that need improvement.

12. Day 13: Learn From Commendation

If there are commendations from the eleventh day, the thirteenth day is focused on improving these acts. An individual can also look at the best way to maintain the good form from the commendations.

13. Day 14: Practicing Empathy

This day is focused on a person being able to listen to other people and being able to relate to them. A person is supposed to avoid being judgmental to other people situation and feelings. It will help a person to relate well with other people. During the process, a person is an advice himself of what he or she would do given the same situation.

14. Day 15: Commending Others

Ann individual is supposed to take time and appreciate people who help his or her achieve his or her daily goal. This day a person can choose to recognize his partner or a work colleague. An individual can open up to how they feel about their efforts in his or her life.

15. Day 16: Fighting Fear Using Knowledge.

A person is supposed to identify situations in his or her life that are influenced by fear. Fear of the unknown has the potential of affecting the normal day to day life of a person. To achieve high emotional intelligence, these fears are supposed to be conquered.

16. Day 17: Learning to Say Sorry

They might seem like the hardest words for a person to say. However, they hold so much power in mending and improving relationships the process is about valuing the relationship and demystifying if one is wrong or right. The day is focused on mending relationships in a person's daily life.

17. Day 18: Learning to Forgive

A person is supposed to forgive people who have wronged him. Learning the art of forgiveness helps a person to move on and heal from stressful relationships. Hanging on resentment has the potential of reducing a person's emotional intelligence.

19: Being Honest

It is the act of being authentic to people about your true thoughts but in a respectful manner. However, it does not entail sharing all personal information. Achievement of this day helps a person to gain respect from other people around him or her.

20. Day 20: Keeping One's Guard

An individual is supposed to have a clear thought to identify people who strike his or her ego. These people tend to push the relationship to the extent a person cannot handle. The process can be slowed after gaining the qualities from the nineteen days. This gives person calmness when things flow at his or her pace.

21. Controlling of Thoughts

It can be difficult to control a person's feelings when he or she is having bad thoughts. However, when an individual is able to focus on these thoughts, he or she can be able to control the outcome of these feelings. A person learns to acknowledge these negative thoughts and move on with an alignment to his values and goals.

Conclusion

At the end of it all this book has come clear in all matters concerning emotional intelligence. Emotional intelligence and all its contents have been explained clearly for everyone to understand. Most people are so ignorant to this topic and thus this book acts as an eye-opener for all to see. Emotions are seen to be connected with human behavior. This is clear during an emotional response. The book gives free coverage for what the book should entail in all matters of emotions and emotional intelligence. There is a deep insight into all the highlighted topics in the book.

The book covers on emotions and empathy and why they are useful in terms of evolution. Empathy shows a sign of growth in a person. One is shown the importance of not being stoned cold. One is taught how to feel for others and also to place themselves in their shoes and not literally. The more one is sympathetic then they are emotionally wise and are not a self-thinker but are more considerate to others. This then helps in making someone easy around people thus making all soft and bubbly. This, in short, says they become happy and contented.

There is the topic on emotional intelligence being more important than mental intelligence. People have put their focus more on the mental intelligence but we see that concept has to change. This refers to the fact that emotional intelligence affects all spheres of life. It helps one build relationships with others, it also shows the job one will take and also the job performance comes in there. All these aspects are shown by emotional intelligence. We all have to agree that all of those are very important aspects thus making emotions very superior and important in life.

The talk of the impacts that come with emotions was also discussed. Emotional intelligence touched so many aspects of life and therefore has so many impacts. It impacts may be positive or negative which is normal in all circumstances. It has effects on the family, relationships, work, friendship and finally one's social life. This is basically someone's inner life or even what others call the inner circle. It does matter the things it brings to the table and how it affects one and others that are around him. One gets that basically every part of life is tapped into by emotions.

Another thing that is discussed is the meaning of emotional intelligence. This may seem simple and like something to be written in five words but it is more. On could look at the specific details that make up emotional intelligence. One could also look at its history and how it came to be known after being ignored for long. It can also be compared to the mental intelligence. One could explain how both work and how different they both are. This section of the book or topic has got all these things covered to the brim for more exposure.

The next thing to be looked into is the emotional intelligence appraisal. This talks about emotional intelligence and the testing that occurs. It also talks about the four components that help in measuring emotional intelligence. This is the understanding of oneself that is one's behaviors and also emotions. The other is being aware of others and considering how they feel when you do something onto them. Another is knowing how to measure one's actions and words especially in the presence of other people thus this is to avoid problems and troubles with people especially those close to you and your life.

The book also dives into the different emotional intelligent test there is. The methods that are there and how they are used is very important in terms of emotion and behavior. The discussed ones are four and each has its own properties and also their advantages and disadvantages. They roughly give one understanding of emotion in human beings and the importance of their measurements. The first is emotional quotient inventory and the next is profile of emotional competence. There is also the trait of emotional intelligence questionnaire and finally there is the Wong's emotional intelligence scale.

The other thing discussed is the emotional quotient. Which is the result after one takes an emotional intelligence test? The chapter should have given the formula to obtain this emotional quotient. This is almost similar to the intelligence quotient the only difference is the aspect which is being measured. On one side emotions are being measured and on the other side it is the mental capabilities of man. You get to see scholars who worked tirelessly to come up with theories and calculations of how to go about in emotional intelligence measuring. Also one see how the results are ranked.

The last thing discussed is the four-week plan to improve one's emotional intelligence. Once one has known how to calculate the emotional intelligence of someone and has known how to rank the result then one should find ways to improve their emotional intelligence. These have been explained elaborately in detail in the book. The first week one works on taming or managing one's negative emotions. It is closely followed on the second week by, having a mindful vocabulary during conversations. The third week is practicing of empathy which shows emotional growth. The final week or week four is understanding one's stressor and bouncing from adversity.

It is important to know and tame one's emotions. Emotions are the basis of one's life they are basically the glue to life. Understanding of emotional intelligence is very crucial to get this life glue to work. Knowing the emotional intelligence of someone is not necessary for just ranking but for understanding emotions in man. Emotions are different in every human being even if they are related by blood or are twins. Everyone is unique in that way. Knowing one's emotional intelligence helps one to know how to improve things and figure them out.

CPSIA information can be obtained
at www.ICGtesting.com
Printed in the USA
BVHW090828220221
600777BV00001B/45

9 781801 861717

WHY LETTER ELLIPSE

WHY LETTER ELLIPSES

KIMBERLY ALIDIO

selva oscura press • chicago, illinois

Published by selva oscura press
selvaoscurapress.com

Printed in the United States of America

First Edition

ISBN 978-0-9909453-5-2

Design and typesetting by Margaret Tedesco
Text set in Neon Block, Gill Sans MT, and Lora
Printing: McNaughton & Gunn

Cover art, Jenifer K. Wolford: *doubledurian, Stage 2* (detail), 2008.
Acrylic paint on wall, 16 x 30 feet. Courtesy of the artist.

Distributed by Small Press Distribution
1341 Seventh Street, Berkeley, CA 94710
www.spdbooks.org

selva oscura PRESS

a 501(c)(3) nonprofit

TABLE OF CONTENTS

ARCHIVE IS TOUSLED

stitch

stitch   I saw seams
          sparrows
          fontanel
                    peonies
a mother wants to know   neither of ours
speak from granite
optimist   I have to get
poisoned by rock   you can't
come with me I don't want to
suffocate

△

          windows
                    cave
          aural temper   I did
say I didn't know
                    how to read
do you agree   under
water clamor   eyes feel
vowel

△

I did sad things   can I take your name
pillowcase   lightly choke
lunge to the cat   silhueta left by death
          survived by   you mean
bedevil   every desire rabbits
time makes miso   comatose calm
I'm particular   only you know
loud in dialogue   or we alone
a democracy

△

          sharp tree geometry
                    my love has certainties
                              washcloth
                              tiny soap cube

does hair
bare skin donned winter
long stretched singular value

△

lifetimes thru the motions natural kill storm
off chemical I'm in your world somehow on probation sharp tone closeness recorded almost infinite I also dislike literary devices! & only use them in impossible conversations as in confession and allegory convey understory weather points interior wordspace at the end of the day the field talks about what it wants enter with gentle ease question sieve soul's biggest story
do not dialogue now
with her the world

△

I am Duncan
Dunparra
coffee and kasha
Birds
stirred for
gay morning
minion's minion
mathemata
Buckle and
present yesterday
excavate pain
tracks and exclaim

△

a pierced deer
plummet I must
scorched-earthing
forest not just lit

"The only thing I will work myself
to death for"

toss into heaps
offenders

△

go to Prune and John's
a nun on a horse
          journey latched to your
winter honeycrisps

△

Pre-visit uncertainty was nice. Fa-
miliarity and dailiness long
distance is not. She's present. Too. I'd give
my dog up for her. Would I regret it.
Would my new love. A calm convener and
diplomat in extremis. Big moves. I've
been working on addiction. I'm not sure
who's listened. I'm hooked on alterity
coming into me. Attempt from love's sick-
ness and fly away. I interrupted
her in my urgency. Since I am my
own fever and pain. How I'll bear tender's
beast. I'd give my dog away to live
in the Village with her and regret.

at the Radnóti

I wanted to
lay my stomach
flat

against the
concrete floor
press

my cheek against
tercets
staggered and

descending
cry on glass a pool
that can't

form in the dirt
below
I desired

the poet's
re-interred force
keening

beauty
salvage our bodily
ground

account for
not those who died
for my

freedom
but at my
expense

My sovereignty
steps
onto the dead

breathing
destroys
in a very plain way

Transfusion via
our mouths
Carolee

Schneemann's *Fuses*
turned me on
even a penis

looks good in
heat maps
Snow doesn't

fall directly but
circles over
your head

imperceptibly
spirals my fingers
inside you

Will you fist me
if I beg in
a whisper

or without sound
subconsciously the way
you said I love you

a dozen times
before you said
it

A doorway unburied
fallen open
to the words

irrelevant illegible

A fist and a flag
are thought to
encapsulate the
dead's discovery of
truth and meaning
especially any
dead interrogated by the
police and
recalled only in
law and census.

Refuge in the
traditional symbols of
our left
makes us powerfully
small
my enemies I no
longer assume are
yours transfixed by
private glories beyond
embarrassment.

My
own revolution this
morning
you quoted Artaud
all action is
cruel push the
limits to
be relevant to
day is to kill
words from the
stage.

At night
traumatized states of
alienation talk
radical slogans
time is now
no other to
aggregate visions
where what words are true
words not myself
own
antidote.

Recall private
language
nectar and blood-
stained sheets is
ethics of
attention to
our cruel hungers
eat their own
tails as a circle of
light.

At the cusp of
dawn a candle on
the mantle
most gorgeous searing
light on mgmt
strategies.

Reckless feeling
attends
a hummingbird before
solidarity fixes.
Which reds are
proper prey for
such a precise
machine.

Official verse
dive bombs informally
around us keepers of
new arcana.

If I've ever become a
book.

I've stopped
being afraid
under irrelevant
illegible light.

low cloud

unfold week
nail paint
iridescent
submit
battle position
perimenopausal
pain
inherited
from mom
baby me
first feels
a woman
turn off Eileen
at the border

cross into
Texas
start a rosary
finger
count decades
three months
since last sex
two since last
face
one since breaking
up
glory wave
cloudbanks
over wherever

home
test proposal
memory
Cherry Grove
in the 50s
new year 1971
brought in
on South Padre
cancel all classes

when can't stop
crying
Sophia conveys
to the café
sit under pendant

deep in
a podcast
foggy swamped
roiling
text Wendy
I don't know what
I'm grieving
hormonal attach
trauma threshold
life habit
keepers
trace
cross-
penetrative

interlocution
epilogue
to the resurrection
treachery
agony
lack of affection
groundless fears
restless
for way out
woman
who inspired Christ's face
to Calvary
last words
grayscale

non-labile need
care still
seethe

routinely
pale scent
draped over
the foot
of a bed
wake up
anyone
loved
wish
others happy
pop song

thank you
notes
bridge repair
procedural
failure
reversals
decide
internalization
or blockage
obstacle or
incomplete
wily sneaky
underhanded
theft

a sacred heart is not immaculate

The cheating hearts of nurses were clean and thorny. In pre-op they clicked binders open and closed. One kept saying NPO and used her phone to remember the Latin. My diaspora took over the late-night shift and entered, one by one, to touch machines. It called me *ma'am* and said we should *baby* the IV port. It was the first to ask, *Does it hurt*? Through the door, it changed a large trash bag with a faraway smile. I was bilious, literally, itchy all over. I sent a floor nurse from the Mountain Province back with news of my parentage. It's spreading, I said to my lover as the door closed. Sure enough, the exiting nurse hugged me and said, *I didn't know! Lita had to tell me!* Above eye-level, Sophia on "Golden Girls" lay on a hospital bed. The anesthesiologist served what he called a *margarita* and later said, *It was a pleasure*. Through the doorway, a woman complained about beautiful healing centers. My lover roamed, found the chapel, and returned with a saint card. She had made gentle pasta the night before, and from the bed I read aloud to her from Wikipedia the difference between the *sacred heart* and the *immaculate heart*. For example: the specialists stood like Superman to declare their procedures, and the nurses let them. Above me, Alyssa Milano transported on "Charmed" to save a woman and I thought, *We are in the aftermath of retribution*. The attending didn't stutter but stood unsure in the doorway.

forever kink

Today an old friend
broke up with me
confessing the kind of distressed abandon
ment hidden in a worry   I'm not myself
I might be possessed   straight
women obsess over boundaried territory
is my gender capture the flag
gift all of yourself is noli
me tangere   number one buzz
look
forever is my kink
a white socks day
plus coconut assam   a gnat or goat   floated in
muffin with a hair
poetics
I want to write a poem with Bernadette's
notebook   now I've told you
is it true
I'm unrecognizable   Gòrecki omens
keep on the frame rather than jut up
furniture
metaphor
on the fly
gutter guitar

underworld underworld underworld

up here someone said I don't get what's expected you laughed
corner of my eye my misunderstanding
is deliberate
"key to the way we live"
Don't try to sway me over

I sent a self-report tried my best with surveillance watched
the watchers and the clock
To your day *on your day*
open to the open casual shaming
I take back under to our home

where broken-open is whole healthy
Your day will go away & intimate
with all of Arizona
a common ritual position tall over lowered eyelids
pagan groom's statuesque form

silt and tidal layers co-corrode
Give me your hand
landed on soft organ
your grunt by my scruff I floated against gravity
and take my hand

sipped long nectar from your center thick ropes
tummy rode down thigh trunk
worshipful
better than anybody's preacher man

blood on a light switch plate
a butch hand swipe after sudden onrush
48 hrs no food feasted on rotisserie chicken dark meat only
stepped-on glasses calmly taped together
spiky black kyanite

typed an email right hand encaustic with blood
wedding wedding wedding terrible shower stall
scene body wash overturned sopping washcloth dripping plosive
blue

archive is tousled

I am dangerous

God’s bird

lick my lover full circle from roof mouth to pussy floor

unsystematic inventory chuckles

no murder today

circus tent domed in new age

over Peking duck
a quick head jerk
can't eavesdrop
lack of tryhard

fascinates
scarification
a planeload
in from LA

certain harm done
whispers constant
processed capital
try make a sound

struggle under 100-lb
plate glass
bloodletter hilt is
a standing human

bathe in activated charcoal
our Olmec dragon
canceled Ansel
down on tasteful jade sun

brother seeks refund
for DNA results
100% circling one
pearl of the orient

dad calls a tall guy
My Bigoted Friend
his statement
signature jewelry

captive mountains
in three rings
sympathy
to crude truth

tweezed-off eyebrows
blank expression
of the tweezers'
gold alloy

godface
shrug
duh lack of
precise tool

rouged boar

a kind question   still tests
          attention   who rats
go ahead
ask me about what I love   someone's answer
a rouged boar   sound familiar

if this were your Project reading I'd come touch your arm
don't panic
          pool lactic acid
cow and cup can be both
entered without a
puncture
           same topology

knot like cup and cow   touch base
                                   or fingerbang
           collectives of words   gun run
                                             from mountain

a white will disturbed *Journal* from its row
I tend   I know   my palate
snug in the graph paper's tiny box
            I know who you are
line by line surprise new souls'
cucumber eyes

                     if this were a sad dinner out
you'd collect sounds of flung down things
case yawn a banana   receive with care
enter a knot   not a line
                       lineage a fancy one
           touch my knee
                      under an untouched dish

my eyes directed to unseemly lines
sound good   gun to back
your careful   his careful
           unlikely shape

my form out the boar
    onto a bed of nails

silence is a cow
a strange plunge   now new souls' cold bath
        one's editorial
        one needs seeing
        one breathes litter on a page

remember to tell a white will never to edit my lines
    or go ahead
I am crying   it read and later I cried
    a long one   men get mean to another
I have to read between

official hours
    suckholes
    one says we're driven mad by madmen with disregard
my former name   nice
    or try to top me   not enough hole

french for horsehead anarchy

not quite a town stutter it's a titty get a ring split the reuben turn
ukrainian Sunday nostalgia into polish courting song solemnly disavow all power but watch

no decent hour for Russ & Daughters
mmmm angelino plums

hail a yellow make quick decisions the clock's permanently off call little ones in their 30s gaybees
queer still nubile hey I'm the ingenue here with ungraded papers
still wet after 10 days

debridement   taptap porcelain tissue
tub wave   french for horsehead anarchy

childhoods spent recounting every liturgical hour hurting
infinitude's feelings box confession isn't confessional on the page

mild frostbite   intense desire
my nap window   white snow   four corners   a void

if you're still lucid and queer after a certain age they'll try to kill your knowing just send
more gaybees
to the hot box up the street

care more about the CIA than care to admit the board cares for language well hallelujah
put in time in a Lyft my golf and The View voiceover

faintly opera   straggling teenmule deer
felt brimmed
rung apple   irrealis neighbor

bodega to bodega
for duct tape
half-n-half and lapsang

critique with even more figuration
I don't hear song lyrics
c'mon say the money number give her the last kare-kare and waffle

dearest, I'm writing from inside this place to you who are in a totally different place

I'm far away. Our bargain – settle on the lowest common denominator.
Geography after all is a modernist romance, a language for how
We diverged from one another. Writing is the fragment of a relation
Made possible by archival preservation and document's promise.

You and I are here to unsettle. Technologies of settling are colonial.
A 1903 language primer gave me my subjective experience of place.
My presumed sphere: pastoral tropics in which play is innocent
Folktales are toothless, a mommy, a daddy and a twin,

A whimsical lyrical chore factory in the object-thing
Of my Malayan heritage taught in English. To teach English
The primer directed us to attune to immediate surroundings.
We were made to perceive and name ordinary objects

Including our bodies. We drew a series of maps. The roads
Connecting our homes to the neighborhood school, our town,
Our province, this archipelago, and, finally, nearby countries.
Objects beyond our field of vision are other houses, towns,

Other children on mountains. Invisible and abstracted are
Bodies of water, other countries and capitals, China and then
The United States – our forever allies! Our particularly childish
Nature of place is the manipulation of scale, size and distance.

Each faraway place was intimate while far enough to expand
Our reasoning and the kinds of felt and flexible relations
within the U.S.-led world. Now adopting the X to acknowledge
Pluralized genders among us moving in this very moment:

Global caregivers, servants, maids, houseboys, sex workers,
Eldercare nurses, cooks, dishwashers, call center operators,
Luxury liner crewmembers. The Global Filipinx fulfills
Basic human needs. The X prosthetic for interdependency.

It is perverse to claim normativity once normativity is
Imposed upon you so that you claim something both

Assumed of you and denied to you? Did you create the good life?
Did you displace anyone? Craig Santos Perez writes new poetic maps

Of the Pacific to make Guam visible. The Philippines shows up
In maps more often than the Marianas do. But still there is a sense
That no one notices when a U.S. warship runs aground of a coral reef.
And once it does it goes into battle position against Philippine park rangers.

That this incident is accidental and yet somehow normal. Like
More flexible jobs in a global chain of military bases.
There has never been one central place in the circuits.
The homeland as sentimentalized as the feelings between employer

And employee. The lowest common denominator between us
Is to be unsettled and unsettling. Place activates our necropastoral
Humanism. We are legacies of exclusion associating us with societal disease.
Yet our families settled. I ask mid-century organizational records,

Why so quietly baroque in your pursuit to become legible, legal
And legitimate? Why so many constitutions and by-laws
For so many micro-interest organizations? I ask a millennial documentary,
Why so full of pathos, drama and claims?

Some go to some kind of traumatized late-capitalist space
A ghost village of fishing families amidst harbor construction
To collage abandoned objects giving us modern perceptions of place.
The problem with the claim that one goes to an archive to find

Oneself is the delusion we can repossess lost property. A place
Is an archive of its own ruins. A place is the archive of trauma
As fact. It happened here. The ships came by to pick up people,
Their cargo and the people hauling cargo. The Pacific is our trauma and

Our desire. The rim is everywhere there has been a war
To get caught up in, always carrying the officer's status in the body
In the closed-door domesticity of empire. Your daily commute through a place,
Your tourist visit to it, your wrong turn leading to it, or

Your binding obligation to stay in it may be a document
Of the place's ruin. You sense the bodies that passed
Through. Flown above. Eaten tunnels into. Exposed brick and oil spills.
Paid out. Locked down. Bodies know more than the curatorial eye

Of the drone or the tight porn shot. The preservationist's weak references.
The developers' biopolitical commitments to life. Ruins and remains
Is a place of present presence, neither passed nor futurist.
You and I here to unsettle.

why letter ellipses

days lunar eclipse sever lines silver dust
                                        why letter ellipses

milky wool steady preference veil   down
the aggressive bed

anger sentiment
coy infant

the antifascists beat the fascists in the second world war is that correct

now for instance in the philippines the americans took over a filipino liberation front called

say the huks to organize them as an antifascist guerrilla group now the minute the fascists

the japanese were beaten then the antifascists reestablished the same

kind of colonial policies in the philippines that the japanese would have put in anyway

the same kind and in fact its worse because the filipinos are much less

interested in having a white man tell them what to do than having a japanese

tell them what to do much less oh there are probably all kinds of antifascists

but what Im saying is that fascism has been made obsolete by america

thats what I said before fascism theres no fascism its americanism

america is the blight on the world

how people moved naked except women with props I crossed campbell slowed eye screeched
arm up to coffee lips savored crosswalk men are horses home to lost skyline

how americans steamed except

subsonic
let everything fall   already crawling
a sunday in new york   at the dutch   man
flee rehearsed in
airbnbs   near the
I-10 and ludlow   cleaning crews
knock   highfee low pay then   the real
thing   terror bedroom neighbor
frats
know your homophobe   landlord
I'm home   wish I could say

you must go

stars interspersed between god and angels everything glittering and gold
church was different from home it had a lofty effect on ones thoughts
levitating latin every trapping was very inspiring

our holy
human energy
sustain our holy
human lives

color mandala flesh no certainty no
what think happened
moral no national tradition
no trivia happened no
why what fools no adult

ages five to twenty I saw startling-looking figures with startling ideas
heads encased in long starched veils ursuline capes when it rained
looked like wraiths

our holy
human energy
telling
the necessary lies

Im not saying there is no fascism
but surely what I know and what Im seeing
at the moment will not inspire me

stream free in a university taught me about blossoming
in the form of nastassja kinski
can't prove harm & good at nothing
a regard kept mannered from life and writing and person

by the very nature demonic
because
its goal is power

always running with great black umbrellas to kill bats literally hanging in the belfry

bewild privacy mistaken for being set free
fire sun rises crackle desire's slate
empty text of singular purpose

very soothing

DEAR ARCHON

origin
and numb
fecundity without
agenda to proliferate

(inhuman life forces that
course through material things to the
immaterial dynamics of all matter and
how they're carried through time)

how you love

(where the ante-normative
persists in being numerous in the
immensity of the constant aeration)

misfiling wonder

object in hand (submarine
super cutaneous areas of unfamiliar
resemblance) order what comes

first what might come
who we had to ghost for

what sticks (when I say ante-
normative it's with a e
it comes first
the normative is after-effect
) drain nature from artifact

artifice and camp
call the future present
before we ease each other
into position

(performative-
to-come)

Autonomous logic. Fragments conditional and grounded in time and space.

What does gathering mean?

What do ordering and completing. Go back like a detective, angle into position, silence and scenery chewing.

Pull the plug, hold for five seconds and throw direct at her.

Utterly absurd. She is very clear about the fact that she was being shot.

Bullet wounds on her body.

Your love betrays. You can't hold the standard of a standard, obstruct freedom of information, toothier conspiracy.

Percentages more spectacular.

Helpless mass of animality. Primal undoing.

Spectacular common sense. On camera blushing.

lapse into shorthand   enunciating   here & there

slack mouth   surprised every time   I ask to clarify   sure

compelled by silent tending   hang around long enough

get in subconscious   already conversing   fluently

homage   supposed to handle   obsessiveness

absorption   don't blame me

I have been thirteen
frowned on   haunted for years
shadow *spread myself*
Cixous   before or after

file my nails in poetry
she hangs in self-absorption
from her lovers   tend to edges
before they tear

unmanageable
palpebral fissure   what threat
clitoris run-on   *slows down*
in Camomille's mouth

plausible surfaces   new
when seen   fingernail
by the italics   higher order
subterranean   *eager astride*

Gravestones too have been taken up and thrown under an ash tree growing upon the lot and some of them are broken.

“300 yards from the Falls Road” “valley of rare loveliness” “the valley floor” “beyond them stretched open fields leading to the wooded Suter hills” “meandered numerous streams”

On an eminence along the turnpike, consists of a cleared field where a number of weather worn tombstones are clustered; most of them have fallen down.

Native Americans, a colonial settler (The Emigrant), a slave planter (The Signer), a Gilded Age robber baron banking and railroad magnate, a robber baron chemist and practitioner of corporate vertical integration, then it was broken up.

Vanderbilt, Wilson, McCormick, McAdoo, McReynolds, Legume, Finance Hope, Purple Knight, Azucar, Matey, Man o’ War, Leslie, Wanamaker, Winston, Eastwick, Shaw, Keith. Laslett, Sarazan, Tilden, Mix, Amory, Baker, Deford, McCormack, Looram, Swann, Mechanic.

“a thirty-mile gallop through three counties from the Chesapeake to the Atlantic” “the semicircle of hills” “nine miles distant” limekiln, mill, potato washing, trout breeding “a spring of pure soft water” “a wide straight avenue of old hickory and scarlet oak-trees” “masonry, marble-lined basins”

On the Falls road, a dark mulatto, about 25 years old, 5 feet six inches high; having one or two of his right front teeth projecting out, very thick lips, speaks very thick and lisps, with a downcast look, shuffles his arms very much when walking, and treads on the out side of his feet, his legs being a little bandied.

Had on when he went away a black fur hat, blue coat, light pantaloons and light summer shoes – had with him also, a light roundabout and two linen shirts. He is disposed to drink and is often intoxicated.

Hunt Cup, Steeplechase, Grand National, Devon, Guernsey, Snowden “post-and-rail and plank fences” Cockey, Sater, Towson, Carroll, Caton, Bonaparte, Chase, Howard, Bowen, Patterson, Wickes, Brown, Coronet, Jonesboro, Add, Problem, Demonstrator, Bosley, Hobson, Field, Palmer, Emerson, McKim.

familiar scandal of ladies
exposing defilement in
delicate thongs

throng
suffocating for details
of human abasement

to end
the most obvious forms of enslavement
we equate it with the obvious

what's owed:
the truth!
runaway tells how rare

whistled greetings
social media persona models
minority shame

nothing not allegory gone viral
pity such offense
help berate

lieutenant gifts
to his twelve-year-old
daughter

costs so cheap and pretty
prettiest booty branches
a graft

we trust heroines
stay pure and just
everyone wounds

love what binds
scrub as if life depends
she recites our ironies

joyful luminous
sorrowful
glorious!

greeting confiteor   (penitential rite)
gloria before the gospel
nicene creed   before diagnosis
martial law visions   Carmelite nun

preparation of the altar
and the gifts
before the preface   sanctus
mystery of faith   refuse dialysis

die   saints stories
piles of grains and beans   signofpeace
congregation hesitates   mahjong
communion

concluding rite   camera
altar   dress with hearts   letter
he's ok   valentine
youyourspirit

andmostgrievousthereforehis   of good will
one pair shoes per child   black dress   veil
mother perpetual help
c-section   worship

we praise you
bless you adore you glorify you give you thanks
three lengths   coconut trees
forest

wooden shoes   o
father
only begotten son   lordgod
lamb ofgod

youyourspirit   at the end
hut   creek   her land
another hut   that is seenunseen
thingsvisibleinvisible

one
in being
consubstantial   sin   two
streets   middle

of the cross   at the end
market   sins   we
I he born   incarnate   died

death   4am provincial
by the umbilical cord hanging
in the house
fulfilment of   accordance

with   worshipped adored
happy   blessed to receive   should enter my roof
youyourspirit

we
acknowledge   I
confess
for forward to   youyourspirit

power
and might
hosts   youyourspirit
this is   behold

State needs Make boundaries bathe in Roses. Absorb their fragrance. Let them connect you To rhythmic pleasure Of the comfort Within.

It is alright if the Lawyer sell the property, we just hope and pray that Inay Leonor even if she is gone be compensated for being a tenant for almost 55 years, even in a little way. But as far as we know, the Lawyer did not honor and acknowledge Inay as a tenant of your property. He said that she was only a caretaker and not a tenant, that's why Inay haven't compensated from other property wherein she is a tenant too.

Consolation in Reliance upon Knowing The B Follows the A. Upset With Lack of Hold Steady. Security is As security Does.

I am sorry if we have disturbed you about these. Thank you very much for your time. We just want to tell you these because it is the request of Inay Leonor before she died. We are not asking for more than what my mother-in-law deserves as a tenant, all we're asking is to please give us a piece of land from this so that we have our own for us to build our house.

Appraise in Tone you'll Freely trade.

We just worried about selling of this 14,000 sq. meter Land, because it might happen again that He will just ignore us. If it is happen, all we have to do is asking him to just compensate us for planting rambutan and Lanzones in this Land. But I doubt if he will grant this request.

birthplace   Susquehannock hunting ground seized in the war
mirrored organs   left and right

molecular inversion of alien and honey   duckface under crown of yellow iris.
flutters a siren call of eyelashes   palm winking hello Bill Nye

born overpopulated with eggs   rhythmic rupture release
former plantation surrounding the port city

fatally shoot a man   who allegedly robbed a Wells Fargo
late summer killing of Korryn Gaines

aerial surveillance   maced 15-year-old on a bike

squat atop our shipped   hollowed keening   diaspora
dead-ends Magellan   riding an ecstatic banana seat

unpatterning unexpectation   secretion via river stream
spikes and falls   sick sea-swells

post-industrial hometown off-gasses   steel sugar
spreads deserts   holocene

Lenni-Lenape burial site   Seven Oaks   an estate
no oak trees left   moveable sacs and crystals

obscure genetic hard pellets   Deren as Rainbow Brite
Mendieta leveling up sacred Atari

planets kneecaps or serenades to the maidenhead

martyr on the Episcopalian crucifix
head cocked to the right
hips to the left double-barreled finger guns
thumbs tucked
mudra sideways
casually crucified
etymologically
scared of what I might do
for you
you never quite satisfy
in the moment
"obviously"
transparent as possible
precarity insecurity neediness fear I already did this
and what have I done
record
what and who I love
imported from actual life
speech act a place
delights a poet from the other side
of town
I'm all ok just let you
have this
I really do
not want to be present
steal
body mass
index by little
vulnerable horror's existential aloneness
no nuance only say it
baby
you are fungible
baby
you called me baby
so soft fascist consensus

I entered names into the record medium place species agent of frustration setting event tree compact portable property intimate & personal love letter flesh hair container physical limit discrete pieces bound together geography compromise circulation

although the law says don't touch Your eyes followed mine in the pink mirrored light

Resonance obligation mutuality glue and engine empire Hopelessly the archon's management of desire grief anger apathy tries to liberate modernization and efficient production Containing traumatic paralysis disavowal requires call-and-response

My eyes held you swimming through velvet smoke two feet away Your reflection caught at the center of my irises the hollows of my palms for piercing

My Vernicle   o La honda herida   or the deep wound
My Vernicle   o Si yo no te olvido   or if I don't forget you
Pa' que me quieras por siempre   To make you love me forever
La consagracion I   the aspirant
spatiality of religious art   lovers without gender   or all men
overlay of face in front of a face   face has two hands   black and white as symbolic meaning
collagraph in 18 parts   spiritual depictions to romantic anguish   this gallery has music
female personal   myth   gender without hair
Abakuá   Perfida   longing

fifteen-hundred-sixty-one miles away from the stomach pit at the edge of a riot years before and decades after my birth sick

of talking with white people about Baltimore leftists who left talking about their comrades who are people who aren't from but talking about mapping the incident and the CVS looting reporting on the Atlantic essay on growing up near living in Cambridge and San Francisco posting on their hometown images restart debates on terminology feed comments that people! are! being hurt! message to stay safe pit of the stomach slack with words statistics white people always taking the mic sick

of the danger that is the city and not the county whatever passes the pit of the stomach where I was born never really from always warned about not the voiced danger I grew up with the places passing through sick

of the cop car and police van anywhere in this country but first and foremost in adjacent to complicit in ignorant of complacent about witness to terrorized by subject to what is said about and done to

displaced from situatedness
dispersed across several continents

there won't be a gathering
finite form embodies the place

where one is now
by indeterminate accident

a desire to mother
a body gains transparency

landscape appears
in a body-framed portal

emplacement of displaced
migrants detained

alien landscape
reconstitutes alien body

what if one makes a new past
body mirror

landscape absorbs alterity
hot-tempered all night

mimetic linguistic
new facts of not-belonging

beyond geospatial mapping
I'm gonna look for my body yeah

I'll be back like real soon

THINGHOOD CIRCULATION

hungers jaw

a story

primes you for   disaster victims
subject to weather
nuclear

in need of rice

but imagine you are a boy
ankles enchant
a light's slant quarter moon

glint

maximalist fantasy projections of high modernist imperialism and fascism used to map a psychic multi-scalar multiverse for my pleasure and aggressive expansion

to dance raving

this proper decolonial poem
dirty with inheritance

support my lifestyle choice or die

a formerly pseudonymous avatar let go
free to wander
sat in a particular chair in a room on a calendar day
flies to NYC holds the baby
smiles to her lover eats
things reads things
writes to the archon resists
market actions
that remain purely market
actions vacuums and contemplates
real consequences of requests
sabotages before beginning
which is gentler than ending
something already in place

keeps her mouth closed
ghosts the institution before it knows
it has a chance
a museum's confused absence
murmurs into an upturned
nothing's face

flying hair
at the top of the water
fishes with wings
what terrible secrets
you hide
we could hardly
hear her
strangling
blissed
finger splay
bird dance
the flock she took
everywhere
ratface anti
freeze blue
babied
three garments
fresh horse chestnut
shone through
a lace coat
murderousness mine
taste all four seasons
lashed to the ship's
berth
with perfume reach
everlasting summer

dinner table end
of dinner
out of her chair
a napkin
followed

a new game
sensorium
pencil on the globe
trains and steamships
real line
spun under hand
we made a ring around
good friend governor
joined hands mercy
have mercy
we laughed
at his funny
accent
gentle ear shake
a little tap
behind the knees
instantly folded
like jointed rulers
we went where
hollowness disappears
a great region for
appetites

we traced chalk outlines

of/
around

islands/
archipelago

obviously a crime
scene

titular possessive (‘s) finger
on

facts earth
in relation
to

child man

big bows at her left ear
funeral
bows on her shoes
open atlas

up soft silver mist
animals almost as strange
as people rushed at him
dad's too quick
for the mad cow
oh carabao
so foul a snort
your fart-face
flung baby
who didn't wail
clung onto
rounded hip
and lived
the style here
horses don't know
they're small
worth looking at
in woods full of bronze
for the mantelpiece
we pierced and
stretched lobes
to store treasures
behind branches
laughed at everyone
bright black eyes
scrambled up trees
scattered in twenty directions

a funny place
to get your girl into
an unseen hand
seized us
earthen floor sunken
like beds to jump on

before you're detained
who is shaking me
I cried
no one someone said
shaking too
I went under
in a second
my dress soiled
in a shower of fish
tangle's little screams
you funny little girl
she said
loosening my net

so many
strange-looking children with such
strange-sounding
tongues
processional torch
costume names
ran into a house
absent of adults
servants in profile tableau
a barefoot boy watering the plants
a barefoot boy answering your emails
a barefoot boy walking cats
mahogany gleamed
bare arms coterminous
with warm curved banister
hip rotators signed half-moons
with half-coconut shells

in whichever
weather event or
greed for candy
babies smoke and swill
coffee
children make themselves sick
everything

they can see
forever coated their
intestines
let me be
your floor polishing
muchacho babe
let me horse chestnut
your fresh lace
I could ten thousand
cocks
strangely tongue
your bamboo
oh tiny horse you
peddling tube rose
little blossom
trees' green canopy
loaded blood berries
night hungry
we hung in my hanging
hair old
embroidery and jewelry
for sale
drank salt sour
never got thirsty again

a girl knows geopolitical strategy

Intricately elegant history of

what she futuristically speaking
cloud formation say

an unfolding expression of
presence recount   very clunky task
extracted words

steps aside the present
back for clues   isolating
turns of phrase

Fragments created by

past selves and strangers   words her bone
structure

arrive   puts her pants on   answers the door
whatever whoever wanders onto the front step
something among her belongings   to offer.

Fragments her body into

someone historical   existence
All actions

require paranoid questions about
her actions   Stats are sculptural

Echoes are rhetoric

Orange is a text   Building is
a poem   These numbers stand for shimmer

a table with five columns

x   today's date   indicators   o

the destination state   A compendium of

phrases in news reports and analyses.

Word for both poverty and pity   Center-justified

list in the thousands and millions
ordered from smallest to largest.

Start with six zeros   Five columns of

numbers   one word "all"
four rows across   not ordered in any way

Strip all but container   Columns   rows
three lines two lines   Arrangement of
identifiers   The hand that compiles.

Arrives at our moment traces of past worlds that give life and death
Church corporation concept
Moon her animal ways
Genetic precondition atavistic selfies the four horsemen
Grammar wet machinery immodest earnings
Medieval cataclysm forecasting Silicon Valley
Opiates use-value of an ear an arm an instep a tool that voices.

Enter foreground hailed clumsily

Social science and siblings called yeoman
    republican virtue and literacy

    unintended rather than handed down weed to seed
    grid serializes lateral to magnificence

New explanation regime objects for observing
    cut out florals real thin

    utility in a wide world of investments hole of the body
    of the story.

Object-perception gets us over diminished thinking-insides
    relative to overbearing unthinking-outsides

    physical surroundings infiltrate the everyday weeds out
    floating dead impersonators leak

Corpses made by machine   machine-made corpse in all kinds of memories dropped at sea
    marinating urine urinating mariner ursa minor guardian   urban marina ruminate Abu Ghraib marine.

Self-diagnosed morphs alters
        boundaries of historical form

With labored breath undoing turns
        reveal what forms

                    With aspiration removes parasitic hope in time

A small mote pressed
        rubbery give suggests carcass   life without history

Reversed the High Priestess spills
        occulted intimacy and desert light

For gesture   the way a hand is placed on a vessel
        the vessel that can never be filled   transport.

Breathe into place   ghost   trope   shadow   nearly feral   mocking ideal twitch
Instigate for adults already knowing rediscovery   remake themselves in rediscovering at
    the edge   the pioneer insists is always the center   the lip of making
    renewal   a retake.

Play circle proves literacy
    Facial muscles convey mapping
Coordinates carry the center to every town stationed
    A cultural distraction

Misdirect to absolute pliability
    Mutually beneficial expansion
Ooze moves the center
    Centers the action catalyzes the edge

Can't spark timely impulse to take on reason
    Barter used goods for new POVs
Hunt for vacant plots on sale
    Crave the raw misprinted extant extinct

Tired of labeling everything unfeelingly
    Collapses at generic human appeals
Corresponds equivalent and parallel to soft power
    Dis-consoles as no one permits

Girl in the geography howling hungry
    A greedily detailed inventory
Happy monster
    Regresses towards the natural claim.

Now the past is a drop in earth an array of survivor an antique shop
The young die to suckle at a cavern's teat

Grandmas weave traditionally bending back sheep heads
Memory an arch of foot reason for a good time

Kids clean knuckles and long intestines
Don't pick your nose

Feint a fake fat yuck yarn
Always animism our matrilineal loom

Shoulder moon-crater of mulched national flower
Pluck variegated acrylic petroleum slake forgetting.

We quarrel in daylight attracting spectators
With our scent and noise

In a district for participating in world news
Unsexed by polar self-interests

Other lovers battle over realizable dreams
Dream us as structural bystanders

Textbooks merely describe from a safe table
Scandalized by loud argument

Empty excuse strives for neutral middle
Reassured that spats break out with bad weather

An amnesiac princess at the door of a room
A housekeeper receives antibiotics from the doctor to smuggle to maquis

Spotted she shrinks back into geopolitical shadow
Correspondence from blue alleys

On the pleasant promise surrounding unpleasant isolation
Refuse to conclude   gape   suck spinal column

Immigration an active life-giving or excretion?
Inflated numbers but marginal phenomenon.

Stop doubting this matters to people not here
There brings creeping obsession and recoil here

Catholic conservative   Maoist leftist   liberal exceptionalist
There and here   allied behemoths at war

Orchestrate rapid response as latticed scaffolding
Circulatory rush.

thinghood circulation

texted I miss you dressed no shower hand
washed underwear next to clean dishes noted
the week's astro met some online training requirement
on info security finished ARK glanced at Celan
ate broccoli cheese tacos
changed into a caftan

△

departed from chance dada defaulted accounts
menaced abjection spirit reduced to instrument trauma
just a formal technique as ableist as intention to make a book
pretty
face

△

autonomous principle listen initiates configure what
trace now mark now what state
offer how-are-you

△

Akilah Oliver did
investigate
which is different than document
remember & forget

△

Ricoeur said testimony becomes a document
under interrogation of a historian
trained in dumb alchemy

△

“restage the encounter of a single consciousness
with text”
come on in
hesitation
delay
funny and vital
runaway
whatever
soma tracks

I'M AFRAID I'LL NEVER GET MARRIED HAPPILY

did you come to the
motherland to eat girls? is a boy's stomach as deep
as a jungle? did you keep your sumptuary limit
in the promise land? do you know how dangerous
you are? how safe you could be?
why not first lick of law? a practice marriage?
any auto-eroticism at the edge of upward
modernity? is society just a hold on your junk?

△

boom
installation in split screen
with the U.S. pledge of citizenship as
subtext
for patriotic oath
which is
more affective?

△

over there
women control one
another on behalf
of men no sense of
their desires once
they as expected re
press so as to ap
pear reserved and
docile don't take ro
mantic attention
personally

△

maybe
someone young
& intelligent to spend 1-2 yrs
in US become americanized then
return home to build
an american bungalow
at the edge of town have 2-3
children only & kiss in public
someone to make over

△

they would say complaining
we don't know her family
& can't
talk with her
daily reminder
reverse colonization
isn't a thing
her ways are not
ours she's american & wife
only secondarily

△

nonbeliever
cannot abide orthodox
shapes of the body
codes of silence
suspension
of impermanence
& consciousness
of such

△

can soft mother protect us in the open? will she terrify
into a demon? order us to remember?
return us against our will
to our assigned time and space?

equivalent
exchangeable "eternal relations
where accounts need not be kept"
dream compound
        (run away with me)
        remainder

△

old restrained life
$25-30/ wk   allowance
get his clandestinely   chaperones
WHY IS IT MOST OF YOU TRY TO CHANGE YOUR NAMES
consciousness of themselves as a product of their experience
WHEN I LANDED IN SF I WAS VERY MUCH IN NEED OF WORK

△

crypto out-in-the-open   filipinos & americans against
chinese money $5/wk for poker parties

patent medicines   rubber goods   silk stockings
masters in philosophy from the university of chicago

△

in 2 yrs saved $2700 $87 to crown a girl
more for a marmon roadster
sold the import-export for $1200
her loss   we're straight with each other

△

tweet uh preach   A REMINDER
"generic criminals"
remains
in force

△

phenomenological crisis   maybe survivors'
guilt   am I or am I not
the NATION

    equivalent boogey
    independent

        collectivize future retrieval
            nether region

absorbed uncertain   destruction   but no
                apocalypse or
    redemption

△

    she's a doctor   knows how to take care
of herself   I haven't said much   except a lot of
endearing terms   I'M GOING TO NY TO GET BACK
    THOSE LETTERS   8am train
arrived Erie 9pm   at a standstill
                while we are going together
                she had to have the abortions
the world is unnavigable   in the present tense

△

                    themselves as
            resources belonging to   an else
            felt   before
            conceptually known as fleeting
            gateways into the foreign
            innumerable unique nexus
            foreign context
                    (out of)

stateless correspondence

an incompetent
under care
average intelligence
a normal sexuality   a normal ability to adjust
to the demands of environment
a good estimate of abilities
a normal responsiveness   to ethical standards

△

a life
of apolitical smallness
so confident

in its importance to history
it unlocks
secrets of power

connected   causal linear   morally
ambiguous as to serve dominant interests

habit of appearing as though we don't
notice much of what we do see

the state is in
bowling leagues
& grandpa things

△

another thing
the bedsheet between us and the past
has glory holes

archive is a jail

one is taken

in harsh absorption into mass
penitence

into

a properly reflexive moment that directly ties memory and self-presence

in the pain of the aporia
never out

graf begets
forget

when things said
tip from the oral field

quest after
us always extra

our ear
psyche our body

historical conditions
feel glyph's open code
material
illogics
power
poly
math
auto
did
act
ero
tics
oth
er
wor
ld
auto
no
my

△

Kusama's bind
    countering
    fascist art-making –

national tradition's
    foreign currency
    earnings

for weapons –
    with precise attention
    to the peony

& O'Keefe's address
    via the US Info Service
    for the global art cult

she kept creating
    uninteresting paintings
    almost devoid

of tonality
    her resistance
    the damnable city

New York
    moving forward
    with creaking noises

american pragmatism
    one could lose
    the phallic panorama

in her compulsive
    repetition of dicks
    & confirm one's

actual existence
        undone by the global
        conspiracy

of total periphery

I was a hello girl

        same old
worldly operations

        night after night
at the railing   stand and sit

watch what is going on
        talk to each other

twirl skirts
kick legs

I've met some
        classy fellows
I'm stringing along

        they can't make me out

                keep on
        forget about me

        spir
        it gu
        t sym
        bol

fallen by the wayside

△

neighborhood　　　always watched
he said one　　　was a charity-assed brod
brought her wristwatch and dress
only two blows struck

show privates
six in evening dresses none cut very low

unable to buy a highball
no liquor on breath　　terrible orchestra music

exceptionally dark
a rotary motion
in masquerade
wide open and rampant

man with cigar
looked like plainclothes

Δ

what does he think
and say? does he talk bad
about me? does he blame me?
tell him to write to me

whatsoever as he has no business
in my affairs
please answer all questions
now for Mark – is he mad?

remember
I wrote saying I was married
but not saying who
please do not give him any information

as I do not know how to spell
his last name
ask him to buy me
some fruit

what's wrong? peeved or what?
you know there really isn't
anything we should be distant
about, is there?
we're an immense field of geo-dots!
no composition at the far edge

△

white as a sheet   and behind him came
this thing   she sat down
in a chair   in her bathing suit   waiting for lunch
to be served
lithuanian woman   once married to a filipino communist
earned $4 a month
left stranded
will chat if bought coffee

△

before long I got to have religious feelings
and wrote poetry to mary
some of it pretty good

I now think I was greatly influenced
by the sisters   they were so much nicer and more refined

if we should chew it blood would gush
and we would die

△

My husband's my god
first he showed me a grand gay time

then taught me
an entirely different way

△

no signs direct the uninformed

IN THE MEANTIME TAKE CARE OF WHAT YOU DO

YOUR PEOPLE
WILL BE JUDGED

△

my back was black and blue and sore for months
it bled some of the time

walked out without getting absolution
None of your damn business

anyway people soon forget dancers
I want to write something worthwhile

sometimes I feel I could kill
for what I see them do

△

early saturday streetcar tracks
to lizards
noir fantasy portraits of poet
POC all-stars + GOP all-stars

my lover has her anti-poetry poem
I announced Bernadette's passing
to the rest of the ex-directors
a nightmare belonging to her

△

some people want poetry that is fiction
what's wrong with poets' lives?
nearly impossible to live

truth-teller
& a kindly person

totally on top of things
an anarchist
in tune with the universe

in times of war people resign themselves to prodigious
extinctions with dusty bravura

I don't know whether to trust the sincerity
or feel provoked by collective perception
free to double back on itself

△

realpolitik recognizes a counter-phenomenology
mobilizing
transformation
across distance
& responds
by asserting a world of only known places

△

Esther at Mike's Diner in Astoria loved my buzz cut & agonized over inconsistent barbers
don't assume you'll get every component of a dish without asking

"That outfit is unacceptable," said my lover of Leslie Caron
closed captions included "[speaking in french]"

marshall plan in allegorical form cleared up confusion about cinematic hetero desire

△

DO WE HONOR THE MEMORY OF WASHINGTON, LINCOLN, HARDING OR
WILSON ON THEIR DEATH ANNIVERSARIES IN THE FORM OF A HILARIOUS
GOOD TIME?

the american teacher made us beat up
a boy to make him come to school
(oral interview inserted into written narrative)
we saw a prostitute at eight years old

brave boys always wrestled jumped each other
market kids roughneck
swore at servants
boys sneered at us in hot water

long hair & long pants at age 16
we were our sister's chaperone
sat down ate when served
inconspicuously watched the ways of people

thus we were introduced to society
fucked our farmworker cousin
& even more servants
hot weather makes us

ready
for this sort of
modernity
sent here

parallel adoption pyramid structure

hid
den
cor
res
pon
den
ces

get us to say

what we know
do what we
do not like

go to bed and get up
and go out
to suit others
stand and watch

bronze statues
remember
ice cream
in our capital city

elite provincial men
excluded
from self-expression
in a global market

run by the US pre world war
post invasion psy-ops
proxies $$$
canon-formation

cia philanthropy
universities moma
poetry foundation

have zero value
as culture
morality history
labor

but provincialism
is the centrifugal
force
of fascism-democracy

wheeled concentrically
location-as-power
a pure geo

politics

testimony
from or about
them

no matter
how excited
renders them
devoid of

tonality

boring as white-
particle nets

This is the testimony of those who know them best who have studied them without that special animus which is so apt to bias our view of those whom we are, for a time, obliged to regard as our enemies.

They live as masses elsewhere.

They stand on the deck of the launch, smiling and raising their hats and waving their hands with the un-Anglo Saxon gesture used in greeting.

△

arrived detached
generic purloined

told my sister to invite her to tea sister told me to walk her home
family invited me in next time I said brother-in-law is her relative
I said I'd marry her in three months went to the city to work
to another province with my sister family sent me here

copy
confiscated ship inventories

200 on the boat picked apples in Yakima Valley car broke down in Joliet
factory work sick leave not hired back made picture frames
Speedway Hospital fired unemployed two years domestic for a year fired $150 savings bought a car

$500 total remitted
since arrival
no desire to return

The butter is always floating about in a tin.

The effort of moving my hands puts me in a perspiration.

Whereallthehorsesaresmall,onelosesthesenseofproportion.

Big lurid clouds.

They always sit down at receptions.Their houses are furnished principally with chairs.They don't understand moving about.

My lady wears a chemise, a yard or so of red calico around her body. She bathes in the surf in the morning.They sit one opposite the other, over a soup bowl and ladle out the liquid with spoons, eating it directly from the tureen.

Small black creatures with no voice so they conceal their intentions until they have bitten.

They may be treacherous, and everyone says they are, but on the surface they are very agreeable.

One strode along with a cigarette in her mouth and a small coffin on her head. Shoulders thrown back, chest and abdomen thrust forward, they march along, ungainly but independent. The majority barefoot but several clatter in wooden clogs.

There are said to be thieves in the neighborhood.

The tales of mildew are beginning to be verified. Shoes fill with mold. The climate is ruinous to books and my leather-covered copy of Browning will be spoiled.

Fields are neglected and overgrown. General impression was of a rather desolate country. The only living beings were soldiers guarding the railway.

They are more impressed by the first shipload of mules paraded through the city than by the troops.

Just as we were leaving a tall "Indian woman" appeared dressed in a straight narrow skirt and cotton jacket. No one seemed disturbed by her sudden appearance.

△

flashy clothes
conspicuous
appear so sneaky and cheap
always criminal or carnal intention

sinister look has been said
too forward
a dirty race

from sailors
run amuck on board

proud to call
an educated one friend

my father fought in the war came to hate

have heard
cannot be trusted statement is silly

the creeps
too stuck-up

tend to knife you
in the back

don't know enough to make a
fair
remark yet I do not want to
have
anything to do with them right
now

△

a new mag gotten
out by "some filipinos &
some colored people"
began April 1932

endeavors to create a feeling
of nationality among the people here
of mongolian and negroid blood
for the purpose of exterminating the white
race

this sounds a little strong
but she seemed unperturbed

copying the masons
secret pyramids of men in the provinces

then the half-educated small middle class

until anticlerical free thought
reached brutal purity among the rest

making $1/ day on sugar plantations
donating $5/mo on independence
raw fruits & veg for new arrivals
15k people on honey & water

readying for an impending revolution
& the great famine

he took my hand and held it   some kind of feeling crept over my body
he took my name and told the congregation

he admitted everything
turned his eyes to the future

hermetics

quest to remember
as above
so below

occulted in
romance

△

how frequently we find in their social
life
demands for consecration
alchemical fraternities
grief for lost unity

birthday party
given by mostly communists
with little prejudice
one of those tours through the westside

30 sorority sisters of the christian social action group
flooded in

an informal party
ready with
extemporaneous speech
ideals
ambitions
agitation

sex work
open marriage

in english with strict parliamentary rules

△

the candidate got after her
said if she didn't love him
& go with him
he would kill her
she came home
& told me

see she has to report to me
every night

he says she has to
she has already been
to his room

△

lost in long halls
I tried to hear
what was said in english

children's cries
a boy just a little over a year old
in a high chair fed rice

some old stores
might be deserted but the door
handles were well-polished
they looked at
folders the size of christmas cards
covered with chinese
characters
I didn't see
any laundry in or out

△

whenever I came in
girls fixed their hair
powdered their faces
at the mirror
boys enjoyed
watching

no stand for the drum
could not get it in the right angle
played it well nevertheless

an elaborate clog

a modified charleston
whirled endlessly

△

he handed me a card

why go to the zoo?

come to the NAIL RACK

people who know too much
about things that don't concern them
or too little

Sun 8:30pm BIG DEBATE
titian-haired terror of the Farmer
Labor Party
vs the effete egomaniac

lectures Weds Sat Sun on everything
from nebular hypotheses to the
the hazards of sex
perversions and hell in general

dancing after
& canvasses on the walls

△

we began with the weather
progressed through the depression to politics
became a little more personal

they talked in dialect
an occasional array of american cuss
words did their counting
in spanish

I took the names down
phonetically

once they believe in you
they will tell you anything
they are suspicious at first
sometimes they will trick you

don't let them know you're investigating

△

They are immensely conceited and believe themselves the center of attention both here and there. "Remember the civilized world beholds and wonders!" Miguel this and Manuel that are celebrated as world-renowned patriots, or as statesmen "steeped in the atmosphere of diplomacy."

They are very polite and desire to be thought men of the world.

The pink, blue, and green little fluttering creatures, bedecked with diamonds, who offered us sickeningly sweet ices and politely asked if we would like a glass of whiskey, were really the ladies in the movement for the emancipation of women.

It is said he has relatives in town who rent houses to the army and send money out to the insurgents in the field.

The town itself looked not unlike Pompeii.

The wives beguile the $$$ from our pockets while our husbands bestow good governments with liberal hands on their provinces. And what shall I do with all the stuff I have bought?

One can never forget the motion of a girl's shoulder as she hitches up her sleeve.

She sits crouched over a fire, her head tied up in a towel, and refuses to understand any language. Clothes brought and laid at her feet and big shiny dollars held up before her have awakened no sign of intelligence in her dirty, black face.

I remember one hot afternoon taking a siesta on a big bed, with three or four placid-looking, plump girls lying on mats on the floor. They knew it meant ruin to them and their family if we abandoned them; they wished them to stop fighting, yet, while they were fighting, blood would tell, and they wanted the insurgents to win.

Δ

no politics
        without conspiracy

        said I
                delayed the police

brains of a gang
raided again
in jail
for the twelfth time

out of the turmoil
trying to fight bees

like women
like women
more to do with women

△

he expressed the internationalist
point of view

appreciated the food prophesied roosevelt's
election czechoslovakian beer within six
months

was currying favor or
honestly converted

furthering his end
with negro groups

△

be careful not to let them feel in any way
you think yourself superior

dress very carefully
each has about six suits

ask for the husband
don't talk with the wife

do not say more than you have to
just let them talk

listen to what they say

don’t discuss independence

△

he tried out bits of his speeches
until shouting from four or five feet away

straightening his body
for all the world
a smaller edition of mussolini

see I organize them   they will not work
unless one orders them about
they will rebel before I finish the job

they are the hardest people to manage in the world

△

a dilemma

never tire of talking about japan’s stance
on a future in which independence
is granted

their pretense is profound lectures
really only interested in where they can get a job

△

at least stop the questions

they will wander in questions all over the world

you haven’t mentioned race
where does that come in

would it lesson conflict if
germany were for the germans

the philippines for filipinos

have you ever noticed
our people always answer
their own questions

△

opened up the lock box
for a letter of reference

tore a leaf from my notebook
asked for his map

KC into rural MO s IL & ne AK
Sikeston Matthews Charleston Birds Point Point Pleasant Canalou
Caruthersville Bragg City Wardell Pascola Steele Hermondale Swift
Armorel Clear Lake

japan to manchuria
italy to ethiopia

for eventual defeat
seer of the thousands

purple cloth for the coming invaders
purple curtains for the salvation army

wives of deportees
party lovers

doctrine of the millenium
dream history

I noticed in the paper you've been stabbed
by a filipino we are interested
in interracial understanding
and that kind of thing worries us

arrogantly
dressed in work clothes
needing a shave
my only regret
is that I did not kill him
I don't want to be
beaten up
just any time

As we could not shut the windows, we were obliged to wash our faces and comb our hair in full view to their intense interest.

She and I went out driving.

It was stifling and unusually hot as the building is in the walled city. The ladies began to show outlines of shoulder blades in perspiration.

Many seem to think the fiesta is a mask for an uprising. We don't believe it but one cannot tell what an excitable people might do and it would be easy to murder us all. Some persons think the rumors of uprising are started by the natives for the fun of seeing soldiers turn out. They said the other night of plots to assassinate them.

All the town is laughing at him.

The sides of the walls were open for air. I heard insurgents whispering under my bed and coming up the ladder.

Things had happened to relatives and friends. She and her sisters fled at their approach and lay hidden for days after burying all their valuables. Their father is one of those who has taken the oath and is not popular.

The children's faces were like sphinxes, immobile as rocks, as if they had never been young and would never grow old. All the dances were similar in character, there was little motion of limb but a snakelike muscle movement.

The streets were thick with dead locusts.

Small brown choirboys ran about constantly reminding one of acrobats as they doubled themselves up like jack knives never pausing in their trot each time they passed the altar.

The figure was of wood and we learned she was a saint brought from an interior town and dressed up in secular garments for the occasion. She wore a purple gown with a deep flounce and had a crown on her head and our flag around her waist.

Costumes that may be said to mark a transition from here to there are ugly.

△

on the streetcar   sat down by him
he hesitated

a new bright blue suit a gold cross in the coat lapel   a pretty tie and a new felt hat

I stopped him to ask where
I could gamble he asked me
what I wanted after I had
already told him   he stopped
to speak to someone in dialect
who asked me again   what
I wanted

flushed & looked straight at me
are you going to publish something

△

word's immanence
descriptor
darker races
translate   secret society
extra to the poem's organizing ground
hunger migration neoslavery
ambivalent about inscription
however fanciful such scenarios might be
how to read the world

precursors to the explosion
of a technophilic Afro-futurism

say a word

a Black
incarnation of
imperial might

federal informant
tipped into testimony
disgustingly fanatical spit

shared descriptors
of reality
proposing
collective

dominion over
worldly ops

freedom of information

George Cruz was   recruited and forced
to pose as a filipino   actually
a japanese restaurant cook
in St. Louis

got him on fraud
under blue sky
law   anarchy
statute

thick japanese accent
a filipino
incarnation of
imperial might

a halo'd cactus spilled from its pot
across my back glochidia
hair-like spines

short prickles often barbed
hundreds per tuft
barely visible
lodged plant material mechanical irritants

memories are general & rather vague
as far as imparting info
with no notebook

lived there a whole month
just to know them

I rifled through the recycling bin
conspiracy of peoples tango with conspiracy of kings
under cover of a psychodivergent bleedingheart

looks like I'm getting interviewed now

metaphysical and masonic fronts for other
worldly operations
by then a long tradition

glochid-hair shirts
charred with butchered latin prayer

my mother could not read nor my father
now all of us can they did that for us
we got to do our part if it costs our life
you should not be afraid to die

how-to diagrams
magic against holy warriors

viral Tucson city council meeting
#greenshirtguy
laughed at #MAGAhatwoman
closely monitored by journalists

imperialism's racial justice
stories of king kong   thin allegories of lynching

now open attack politics drop predecessors' politesse
coding killer intents
innumerables
taken
children
of the took

gallons of water
outside its limits read as
criminally abandoned
property

sanctuary city
vote

memory as key to subversive origins
neighborhoods engulfed in dream history

invasion might bring
swift end to the seemingly endless division

occult terrain
out-of-this-world

CODA

Docupoetry? I was a historian first.
Or second.
Never at the same time

    maybe a few years of overlap
    maybe just at the moment?

which has something to do with *form*

    not *discourse*
    although I might really mean *discourse*

the aesthetic experience of reading and writing the historical study

    the argumentative and over-cautiously cited narrative

within the closed circle
of historiography

    all the reading and writing
    by everyone in the field
    both living and dead.

On the surface, historians are like poets

    fusty

but more incrementally authorizing anything new.
One with the sluggish pace of institutional responses.
In that way, so self-effacing

    almost occult

seeing little difference between the living and the dead

    ideological zombies
    redeemed by peer review
    like white-supremacist anti-black hypernationalists
    resurrected in every lit review on the Reconstruction.

A primal scene:
my first-year PhD seminar on a Nicholas Lemann book

    can't remember which one

on a journalist who attempted our craft:

Is it watered down history
published in a trade press?
Did he oversimplify the Great Migration
for the popular reader?

    Although, a decade later, my department cynically recommended
    we write op-eds on what *history will tell*
    to appear relevant to a legislature paying our salaries.

I came in with a cohort of twenty
after ten years only five got hooded
only five were sentenced to six years
probation to tenure.

O peer review! The anonymous reader's note
scolded me for failing to engage
a golden boy who asserted *rigor*
against decolonial approaches like mine
in a 300-page book that essentially said nothing new.

I meander into conspiracy theories here:
the veneer of boring inconsequence
obscures the real records
all the while demanding we show our papers.

In my medieval churchlike apprenticeship
I did what I could
to get inside
read the *document*
against the grain

    for the classificatory systems directing how to read
    temporal measurements, geopolitical fantasies, aural quantities

but I secretly read the *document*
as a vernacular
occasional poem

bodily inscriptions
of presence and perception
in moments of open aesthetics
responding to

impractical constraints of
colonial *discourses* of space and time

sly workings of official language
casting U.S. colonialism as the opposite of what it was –

a militarized for-profit dictatorship
in the name of pro-nationalist democratic tutelage –

to set into motion invasion and homegrown dictators
maintained by systems of perception,
space, time, identity.

Another anonymous reader's note
full of exclamation points declared
neither *document* nor historiography
could reasonably lend themselves
to interpretations like mine.
Advice for the minority historian
who might appear biased

writing veiled memoir not history.

History is really an invitation
by way of arranged language
to read the occulted
in plain sight:
a poem.

This book is a commingling of archives

with copious attributions
without peer review or a known market.
A history in which the *document*
is contemporary nonfiction
represented in verse

> language's contemporaneity taken back
> from archive-as-Empire's governance

and my poem journals are archival.

> "Give me some mundane details of your day"
> asked late-morning missives from Missoula to Tucson.

Much of it a joyful rip-off of her *A Year from Today*
not only its sense of sound and line, use of caesuras
citation of poets and artists, vital attunements
but also: "it's true/ you have to become your own historian."

△

The historical form remains
the esoteric mediator
between an average person and the *document*.

> Although most anyone can walk into the National Archives
> it's a lot of bureaucracy and why would you
> unless genealogy is a hobby.

There's gatekeeping in the fustiness
restricting any fevered touching of preserved decay to zombie dads
and poet moms.

The historical form is burdened memory. A field
constrained by its patriarchs
a chorus of enforced consensus and increments

> still
> the
> shadowy authority

sheltering documentary poetry.

What poets annotate and cite in the backmatter
a point of departure
somewhere between overcitation and "I'm the first ever."

A documentary poet is
a user of the past
even if she inverts historical objectivity
for decolonial, experimental somatic poetics.

Self-referentiality won't help
if the dead
are empty screens

for the poet's projections
of her postcolonial body

performatively supine

the only one left alive
in the quest for remains
under the spell of counter-exoticization.

What's affecting and close-at-hand
are temptations of immersive trauma

eyes in the trees
eyes in the trees!

But whose?
The *document* is
an antidote to
any art or writing
solely serving a cult of personality

singular or collective

in the death-drive pursuit of pcwer.

Some dead do not speak in the archives.

Some living do not speak in our presence.
What then is the reality of any presence

imprinted upon
wolves, trees, a
missionary, photo-
grapher, filmmakers,
a poet, readers
of missionary text,
readers of a U.S.-based
poet
– beings & forces
organized contingently
fluidly, dynamically
around figures
who
have stories
not reducible to
the moment of
discovery
fixed there
by the
missionary
conquistador
in aphorism
and enumeration.

This has always
been the way, since the
Church sent out its best
rapists. Can I say this?
I do.

Estévanico "the Moor" "the Negro"
was a captive collaborator.
If he had spoken in a way that could reach us
what syntax
would he use? What forms?

The *document* is
an antidote to

history
anecdotal
to stories everyone already knows.

> No argument, source or method will undo the event of silencing indifference
> leading us to believe we can't read anything without clear directions on how.

Once read, it slips back
into insignificance.

A docupoetics might desire to be disoriented
by a captive improvising within a conquest narrative
to experience language
as a medium of consciousness

> collective and singular

rather than gather
evidence
of some meaning
someone is burdened to impart.
Labor and demand
time to hover in a convergence
to relearn how to exist
in and beyond this world.

NOTES

Archive is Tousled

John Dryden, "I Attempt from Love's Sickness To Fly"; Henry Purcell, *The Indian Queen*, Z. 360.
Gerard Manley Hopkins. "The Windhover."
Stacy Szymaszek, "Fun Meter" in *Famous Hermits*, forthcoming.
Stacy Szymaszek, *hart island*, New York: Nightboat, 2015.
John Waters, "Cancel Ansel" at the Baltimore Museum of Art, Oct 7, 2018 - Jan 6, 2019.

Dear Archon

Amiri Baraka's talk at the Overseas Press Club, February 17, 1965.
Lara Cox, "Reaching for Archive Fever: A Tall Tale about Queer Made in France." *Paragraph* 39: no. 3, 2016: 319–334.
Andrea Dworkin, *Woman Hating*. New York: Plume, 1974.
Jacques Derrida, "Archive Fever: A Freudian Impression," trans. Eric Prenowitz, *Diacritics* 25: no. 2 Summer 1995: 9-63.
Exuma, "22nd Century," as sung by Nina Simone, 1971.
Furio Colombo's interview with Pier Paolo Pasolini, "We Are All in Danger," November 1, 1975.
Adrian Heathfield, "Afterlives: The Persistence of Performance," September 25, 2015, Museum of Modern Art., New York.
Susan Howe's interview of Bernadette Mayer, April 22, 1979, *PennSound*.
Fred Moten, "Blackness and Nonperformance," September 25, 2015, Museum of Modern Art, New York.
"NKAME: A Retrospective of Cuban Printmaker Belkis Ayón (1967-1999)" Scottsdale Museum of Contemporary Art in Arizona, Oct 30, 2018 - Jan 20, 2019.
Alice Notley, "At Night the States."
Miklós Radnóti, "Root," transl. Zsuzsanna Ozsváth and Frederick Turner, Holocaust History Center, Jewish History Museum, Tucson, Arizona.
Solange, "Weary," *A Seat at the Table*, 2016.
Alex Tizon, "My Family's Slave" *Atlantic*, June 2017.

Thinghood Circulation

E.D. Aguilar, Director of Public Welfare, Manila, to Charles Burnett, Chief of the Bureau of Insular Affairs, March 11, 1938; General Classified Files, 1914; General Records Relating to More Than One Island Possession; Records of the Bureau of Insular Affairs; Record Group 350; National Archives Building, Washington, D.C.
"An Appeal to Reason" *Filipino Student Bulletin* 3: no. 4, February 1925: 2; Box 1245 Entry 5, Folder 27698; General Classified Files, 1898-1945, 1914-1945; General

Records Relating to More Than One Island Possession; Records of the Bureau of Insular Affairs; Record Group 350; National Archives Building, Washington, D.C.

Ernest Burgess Papers, Box 130, Folders 5-9, Special Collections Research Center, University of Chicago Library.

Frances Williston Burks, *Barbara's Philippine Journey*. World Book Co, 1913, 1924.

Rafael Fernandez, "My First Days in the United States" *The Philippine Herald* I: no. 2, December 1920, 52; General Classified Files, 1914; General Records Relating to More Than One Island Possession; Records of the Bureau of Insular Affairs; Record Group 350; National Archives Building, Washington, D.C.

Filipino Pioneer 1: no. 9 , an. 25, 1937,; Library of Congress.

Filipino Student Bulletin 3: no. 4, February 1925: 2; Box 1245, Entry 5, Folder 27698; General Classified Files, 1898-1945, 1914-1945; General Records Relating to More Than One Island Possession; Records of the Bureau of Insular Affairs; Record Group 350; National Archives Building, Washington, D.C.

Filipino Study, Interview Documents; Folder: Reports; Department of Research and Survey Papers; Special Collections, Chicago Theological Seminary.

Juvenile Protective Association records, Folders 104-105, Special Collections and University Archives, University of Illinois at Chicago.

Bernadette Mayer on "A Close Listening with Charles Bernstein, September 13, 2007" *PennSound*.

Edith Moses, *Unofficial Letters from an Officer's Wife*. New York: D. Appleton, 1908.

Albert Gardner Robinson, "The Real Filipino" *The Independent* 52, 2707, Oct 18, 1900: 2489.

Vince Schleitwiler, *Strange Fruit of the Black Pacific: Imperialism's Racial Justice and Its Fugitives*, New York: New York University Press, 2017.

Daniel Widener, "'Perhaps the Japanese Are to Be Thanked?': Asia, Asian Americans, and the Construction of Black California," *positions* 11: no. 1, Spring 2003: 26.

Midori Yamamura, *Yayoi Kusama: Inventing the Singular*, Cambridge, Mass.: MIT Press, 2015.

ACKNOWLEDGEMENTS

Thank you to the editors who published pieces collected here: Alexis Almeida for *Folder*; Anselm Berrigan for *The Brooklyn Rail*; Claire Bowman, Schandra Madha, and Annar Veröld for *I Scream Social Vol. 2*; Ching-In Chen for *Texas Review*; Clarity Haynes for *Altar-ed States*; Janice Lee for *Entropy*; Saretta Morgan, Marta Lucia Vargas, and Amy Sara Carroll for *Aster(ix)*; Marthe Reed and Linda Russo for *Counter-Desecration*; Janet Squires-Duffy for *Boston Review*; Stacy Szymaszek for *midhriff*; Eileen Tabios for *Puñeta*; and Michelle Tudor for *wildness*.

Thank you to readers who supported these poems, including those in various workshops, and: Chiwan Choi, Gabriel Dozal, Janice Lee, Farid Matuk, and JD Pluecker. Thank you to Susan Briante for encouragement on the entire manuscript.

Thank you to Fred Moten for his generosity as an editor and, more than anything, his friendship over the years. Thank you to Ken Taylor and selva oscura. Enormous gratitude to Margaret Tedesco for the book design. Maraming salamat to Jenifer K. Wofford for lending her artwork for the cover.

This book is in intimate conversation with Stacy Szymaszek. I thank her for the generous and generative poet she is, for the subversive knowing in her poems, and for her companionship and love. This book is for her.

KIMBERLY ALIDIO is the author of the poetry books, *why letter ellipses* (selva oscura), *: once teeth bones coral :* (Belladonna*), and *after projects the resound* (Black Radish). Her most recent chapbook is a *cell of falls* (Portable Press at Yo-Yo Labs). Her prose has or will appear in *Harriet Blog*, *Poetry Northwest*, *Social Text*, *American Quarterly*, and the anthologies, *Counter-Desecration: A Glossary for Writing Within the Anthropocene*, and *Filipino Studies: Palimpsests of Nation and Diaspora*. She holds a MFA in Poetry candidacy at the University of Arizona and a PhD in History from the University of Michigan. (kimberlyalidio.com)

Other books from selva oscura press

Alameda by Broc Rossell

Mood Indigo by Jeanne Heuving

Veronica: A Suite in X Parts by Erica Hunt

Eroding Witness by Nathaniel Mackey

afterKleist by Matthew Fink

A Spell in the Pokey: Hugh Walthall Selected Poems Edited by Aldon Lynn Nielsen

Zippers & Jeans by J. Peter Moore

Moment's Omen by Nathaniel Mackey

dog with elizabethan collar by Ken Taylor

And by Three Count Pour
(an imprint of selva oscura press)

No Hierarchy of the Lovely: Ten Uncollected Essays and other Prose 1939–1981 by Robert Duncan
Edited by James Maynard

Songs In-Between the Day/ Offshore St. Mark by David Need

—Durham Suite: 5—

Anuncio's Last Love Song by Nathaniel Mackey

Southern Colortype by J. Peter Moore

first the trees, now this by Ken Taylor

A History of Fire by Dianne Timbin

[Distressed Properties] by Magdalena Zurawski

selva oscura PRESS

selvaoscurapress.com